P9-DFD-805

Twayne's United States Authors Series

Sylvia E. Bowman, *Editor*

INDIANA UNIVERSITY

Edgar Saltus

EDGAR SALTUS

by CLAIRE SPRAGUE
Brooklyn College
City University of New York

Twayne Publishers, Inc. :: New York

Library of Congress Catalog Card Number: 68-20811

MANUFACTURED IN THE UNITED STATES OF AMERICA

Preface

THE LIFE AND WORK of Edgar Saltus is rich in its suggestions of analogues and parallels in American and European literature, history, and philosophy. What his career suggests about an American like himself in the later nineteenth century may be more important than his actual literary corpus. If I have suggested far more than I could develop about such analogues and parallels, that is my reason. These suggestions may support other students who have found the period unexpectedly diverse and self-critical.

The curves of the Saltus reputation reflect reasonably well the shifts in literary taste in the United States since the 1880's. Chapter I briefly examines the pattern of rise, decline, rise, decline which marks the Saltus reputation before proceeding to the life of Saltus as a son of New York. The appropriation of Schopenhauerian pessimism described in "I Am, Therefore I Suffer" demonstrates Saltus' need to construct new underpinnings for his criticism of the self and society. Chapter III examines the Saltus novels as exampla of ornamental disenchantment; Chapter V turns to his scattered literary criticism, significant, not because of its depth or extent, but because of its central involvement with the French example. For Saltus, as for James Gibbons Huneker, France was "la patrie psychique."

Chapters IV and VI discuss two complex and still relatively underdeveloped questions: the meaning of style in the 1890's, its possible connection with the revolution of prose style in the twentieth century; and the close correlation between Eros and violence. In Saltus, violence and crime exist as themselves and also as definers of history. Between the historian and the amorist in Saltus there is a connection, the full nature of which I have not analyzed. Nor have I more than suggested the relevance of such a connection in the history of Romantic and post-Romantic literature.

Perhaps this study and the forthcoming re-issue of Saltus' works will bring to Saltus a more secure public and place.[1] He may not find "the definite niche in American literature" Carl Van Vechten expected him to find, "somewhere between . . . Edgar Allan Poe and William Dean Howells," but he may leave at last the list of our illustrious obscurities.[2] The Spanish literary historian would place him easily in the "periodista" tradition, making him less "illustrious" but more potent and certainly less obscure as a writer than his countrymen have.

I am indebted to Elsie Welsh Saltus for the pleasures of her company and cooperation and for having allowed me full and free use of her Edgar Saltus collection. Without her care, the collection of her father's works would not exist at all; without her special visit to the United States from residence abroad it would not have been unearthed for years. Now, by her generosity, the collection is at Yale University where Edgar was once a student and where Norman Holmes Pearson and Donald Gallup favored Elsie Saltus and myself with meetings invaluable and delightful. I am grateful to Elsie Saltus and to Yale University for permission to quote from unpublished materials.

I wish to thank Raine Edward Bennett who helped me to locate Elsie Saltus and those who shared with me their knowledge of Saltus: Samuel Loveman, Charles Honce, Seymour Saltus, and Eric McKitrick.

I owe much to many friends. I must, however, single out Warren Susman, who read and criticized the manuscript; Dr. and Mrs. Irving Schneider suffered similarly for me. To Sylvia Bowman, who suffered most, I owe rigorous and thorough editorial criticism. Finally, to Frederick J. Hoffman, who taught me, I credit what is best in the book.

A grant from the American Philosophical Society made extensive travel and research possible. It is a pleasure to be able to thank the Society publicly for its assistance.

CLAIRE SPRAGUE

Brooklyn College

1. The Bibliography, pp. 145-6, stars the Saltus works being reprinted by the AMS Press, Inc., 56 E. 13 Street, New York, N.Y. 10003.

2. "Edgar Saltus: A Postscript," *Double Dealer*, II (October, 1921), p. 164.

Contents

Edgar Saltus

Chronology

1855 Edgar Evertson Saltus born October 8 and baptized June 24, 1856, in the Dutch Reformed Church, New York City.

1871-1872 Attends St. Paul's School, Concord, New Hampshire. Enters class of 1876 at Yale in September, 1872. Leaves at the end of the first term.

1873 Returns to Yale with the class of 1877. Remains until Christmas.

1873-1878 Tours Europe with his mother. Studies in Paris at the Sorbonne and at Heidelberg, and Munich.

1878 Enters Columbia Law School.

1880 Receives law degree from Columbia.

1883 Marries Helen Sturgis Read, daughter of a banker, November 28, at Grace Episcopal Church, New York.

1884 Publishes his first book, *Balzac.*

1885 Publishes his first study of pessimism, *The Philosophy of Disenchantment.*

1887 Publishes his first novel, *Mr. Incoul's Misadventure.*

1889 Death of brother Francis on June 26 at Tarrytown, New York. Publishes third novel, *A Transaction in Hearts.*

1891 Divorce decree from Helen Read granted June 18. Completes *Imperial Purple.*

1893 Engaged to Elsie Welsh Smith, granddaughter of John Welsh, once United States minister to England. Association with P. F. Collier begins with contributions to *Once a Week.* Marks the beginning of his journalistic writings, which are especially heavy during the later 90's.

1894 Marries Elsie Welsh Smith in London, December 17.

1897 Daughter Elsie born, November 27.

1901 Mrs. Saltus obtains a separation and retains custody of daughter Elsie.

1907 On one of his frequent returns from Europe settles for awhile in Coronado Beach, California.

1909 Elsie Smith Saltus dies in Paris. Daughter Elsie returns to New York in the custody of her aunt, Josephine Chandler Smith.

1910 Decline of creative power. Illness. Writes booster articles for San Francisco and Los Angeles papers. Theosophical doctrine appears in his works.

1911 Marries Marie Giles, August 16, in Montreal. Writes articles for *Harper's Bazar, Smart Set* and other magazines.

1914-1918 Writes numerous newspaper articles in support of the Allied cause.

1917 Daughter Elsie Welsh Saltus marries James Theus Munds on October 25 in St. Thomas Episcopal Church, New York.

1921 Death in New York of nephritis on July 31.

1925 Marie Saltus publishes *Edgar Saltus: The Man.*

1923-1926 Posthumous works published, including the novel, *Ghost Girl* and a collection of poetry, *Poppies and Mandragora.*

1960 Death of Marie Saltus, March 20, in Los Angeles.

CHAPTER *1*

Toward the Non-Legendary Man

There is no private life which has not been determined by a wider public life.

GEORGE ELIOT, preface to *Felix Holt*

MYSELF

Not large, not small. Age twenty-nine.
Born in New York. Complexion fair.
Features not altogether fine.
Eyes rather dark, and ditto hair.
Does not believe as Christians ought,
The lore and legends of the Jews.
A dangerous pessimist, in short,
Accused of commerce with the Muse.

Poppies and Mandragora

FEW READERS know Edgar Saltus. Those who do are likely to be fervent supporters who have, probably without being aware of it, accepted the judgment of the 1920's about the pattern and character of his reputation. To critics of the 1920's Saltus was one more victim of the puritan and the philistine; they assumed his early success was extraordinary and short-lived. He became too "wicked" and, after his divorce, personally vulnerable. In fact, we know relatively little about Saltus' early reputation; and what we do know suggests early but not a spectacular success. His journalistic writings through the 1890's and the early 1900's also suggest a continuing though diminished reputation. The lowest arc of his reputation probably occurred between 1905 and 1920, when complaints were heard of neglected genius and when Brentano's began to re-issue his works which were long out of print.

His contemporaries probably appraised Saltus more justly—as an original and lively talent—than did the critics of the 1920's who were so eager to discover examples of neglected genius, partly out of generosity, but more urgently out of their need to provide examples of American cultural failure. Their eagerness was often extravagant but also useful, for it embraced and recovered, or discovered, figures like Herman Melville and Emily Dickinson and also gave a far wider public to writers like Walt Whitman and Henry James. The extravagance, not unnaturally, could not sustain the reputation or revival of Edgar Saltus. To the decade that defined the trajectory of the Saltus reputation in terms of its own subjective needs, the "wickedness" of Saltus inevitably soon turned tepid.

Lesser critics like Elbert Hubbard and Benjamin de Casseres did not help Saltus much when they called him "the best writer in America—with a few insignificant exceptions" or found him "so great that he is unpleasant. He is as unwholesome as truth."[1] Not all his admirers indulged in the turgid and the hyperbolic, for others, more judicious and well known, include Arthur Symons, James Huneker, and Carl Van Vechten. George Moore and Oscar Wilde expressed their admiration more briefly or more privately.[2]

The effort to uncover an Edgar Saltus more in accord with the man who lived is impeded by misinformation and lack of information. Sadakichi Hartmann assured his readers that the Saltus inner sanctum was hung with "Chinese hangings, Japanese screens, and East Indian statuary" over which Saltus presided "on a sort of baldachined throne, much higher than the divans of his guests" to whom he would read Chinese poetry and lecture on Oriental art between puffs on his ten-inch cigarettes.[3] Hartmann's lively imagination saw in the Saltus who walked several cats down Broadway (presumably in the Columbia University area where Saltus then lived) the American analogue to Gérard de Nerval, who led a live lobster on a silk ribbon down a Paris boulevard. The Saltus that Hartmann created does not correspond very well with the man who left so few personal belongings at his death. If Hartmann's Saltus existed (and Marie Giles Saltus denied that he did), he did so long after his best works were produced. Yet many Saltus fans persist in accepting a press agent's dream of what wickedness and exoticism were like in the foremost figure of the American 1890's.

Other errors are merely factual. Gorham Munson believed Saltus wrote his Balzac book at eighteen; Mencken believed he studied at Eton;[4] and, as late as 1925, Harry Hansen of the Chicago *Daily News* believed Saltus had died in 1919: "When he died in 1919 many looked up in surprise, thinking he had passed with the 1890's."[5] Indeed, Saltus' own sense of his final isolation is nowhere more touchingly revealed than in his exchange of letters with Carl Van Vechten during 1918. He is genuinely and wonderingly moved by the latter's interest in him: "You are very exhilarating. I thought my books were sacred. No one ever touches them."[6]

The simplest biographical details are frequently uncertain. About his childhood, adolescence, and young manhood we have no direct evidence. Critics could not even be sure whether Saltus was born in 1855 or 1858. The published family records and Saltus' own testimony supported 1858: but his third wife, Marie Giles, on the evidence of a family Bible she either saw or possessed, argued for 1855. She was right, as the baptismal records of the Dutch Reformed Church show.[7] Whether Saltus made himself three years younger out of vanity, as Mrs. Saltus suggests, is less important than the previous uncertainty; for the uncertainty is symptomatic. Too much about the life of Saltus in his early, his crucial, his most creative years is either uncertain or unknown. Writers of biographical accounts have been forced —or, more accurately, they have allowed themselves—to lean too heavily on the biography of Marie Giles Saltus (?1883-1960), his wife for only the last ten years of his life (1911-1921). Even if we add the number of years of her probably close association with him, ten more at the most, we are still past the Saltus creative peak.

When *Balzac* was published in 1884 Saltus was twenty-nine

and Marie Giles was one year old. His best work ended in 1892 with *Imperial Purple.* He was thirty-seven and had been divorced from his first wife for one year. (Marie Giles was nine.) The avant-garde of the 1920's considered itself sophisticated in psychology (it discovered Freud); but it swallowed almost as gospel the biography by a wife who knew Saltus in his decline, in illness, and who knew his past as an older man told it to a woman twenty-eight years younger than he.

Obsessively preoccupied with animals and theosophy, she told the world at length how well she had transmitted these preoccupations to an Edgar made to seem, in a not uncommon reversal, many years her junior—an Edgar distinctly in need of maternal and sometimes condescending care. This, in essence, is the petulant, shallow Edgar Saltus whom Marie Giles Saltus presented to the public in 1925. Nothing more certainly blighted the revival then in progress. For example, H. L. Mencken, eager to support writers ignored by the bourgeoisie—and once, therefore, a supporter of Saltus as a harbinger of the 1920's, "leading the way out of the Egyptian night of Victorian sentimentality"—but more recently dubious of his value, was, with the publication of Marie's biography in 1925, certain of his superficiality and inconsequence. His estimate is devastating: "I can recall, in literary circles, no more complete collapse." What ailed Saltus "was simply lack of substance."[8]

With Mencken's philippic, given his critical leadership in the 1920's, the Saltus revival ended. The quality of Saltus' work may be frail, but it has something to tell us of the state of the writer and of writing in the United States in the 1880's and 1890's. Saltus, who began with everything seemingly in his favor—birth, wealth, wit, looks, and education—made an impressive start and collapsed too quickly. To say, as Mencken does, with the easy condescension the present so frequently adopts toward the past it simplifies, that "He could be clever, as cleverness was understood during the first Cleveland administration," may not be enough. We are faced with the always interesting case of disparity between promise and achievement. If we take that general disparity and give it particularity within a person placed in a time in American history generally considered a dark age for literature and for the literary life, we have a question sufficiently textured to deserve our attention.

I *The New Yorker: Origins and Development*

Edgar Saltus may make more sense as a son of New York than he does as an embodiment of decadence. He was born to Eliza Howe Evertson (1832-1899) and Francis Henry Saltus (1826-1905) in New York City, probably at 36 West 19th Street. He was descended on both sides from Dutch and Scottish and/or English ancestry. The Evertsons may have adopted Evertson, the Dutch form of MacEvers, when they emigrated to Holland in the sixteenth century to escape religious persecution. Or the family may be descended from the brother of the Admiral Cornelius Evertsen, who took New York from the English in 1673 and later retired to South Amboy, New Jersey.

There had been Saltuses in New York City since 1789 when the colorful Solomon Saltus (1745-1834) abandoned his native Bermuda and his life as the master of a sloop for a less exciting shore life, first as ship chandler and later as an iron merchant in lower Manhattan. Solomon had experienced capture and plunder by a privateer on his West Indian run before he shifted to trading between New York and Charleston and then entirely gave up his career at sea. The Saltus family (the name may be a corruption of Salter or Salters) soon intermarried with the Dutch-descended families of Solomon's adopted city.

Edgar's grandfather, Francis Saltus (1774-1854), continued the mercantile enterprises of his father; in fact, what wealth the family had seems to have been accumulated by him. His obituary was a eulogy to a leading citizen who had commenced "mercantile pursuits at the early age of thirteen years" and had become at twenty-five one of the leading New York merchants, "owning and sailing vessels, the number of which afterwards was largely increased." The details of his commerce with Russia and the rest of his career deserve fuller quotation, for the style and the approach of the obituary, from the New York *Evening Post* long edited by William Cullen Bryant, reflect the era of personal journalism and recall the period beautifully. Furthermore, the facts of the grandfather's life are in striking and instructive contrast with the grandson's:

> "His trade with Russia, before and after the War of 1812, was alike princely in its arrangements as it was profitable in its results. His brother Nicholas, then residing in Russia, enjoyed the

friendship of the Emperor Alexander. When Moscow was burned by tho Russians Mr. Saltus lost one thousand boxes of sugar and an immense quantity of tobacco, and his three vessels, the 'Nancy,' the 'Hudson,' and the 'Bolivar,' were taken by the French on their way home, after successful voyages, for which he never received any indemnification. The high prices, together with the protective feeling in favor of home manufacturers, caused Mr. Saltus to engage largely in the production of iron in his native state; and in this, as well as all other business matters, he proved himself equal to the matter he undertook. He made a wilderness a paradise—an unknown spot, celebrated for its mineral wealth, developing an entire county, leveling mountains, razing forests, struggling through bad periods and changes of the tariff, seeing his works twice destroyed by fire and once by freshet, laboring under difficulties that most men would have sunk under. He seemed to wish to be placed in difficulties that he might have opportunity to extricate himself."[9]

Francis Saltus left, we are finally told, " 'to his children a spotless character, an honorable name, and an ample fortune' "—and, above all, the knowledge " 'that in Jesus Christ he had a friend who did not desert him'." He also managed to accept an appointment as an ensign in the New York Militia in 1796 and to elevate himself to the rank of lieutenant colonel in command of the 3rd Regiment of Artillery by the time of his death. Unfortunately, Edgar never knew his indomitable grandfather, who died at eighty during the year before Edgar was born.

At fifty-two this grandfather, perhaps the most remarkable of the Saltuses, sired Edgar's father, Francis Henry who inherited the vast acreage in the Lake Placid area of New York State, the source of the iron ore sold at 7 Beaver Street, and who also continued the traditional shipping and iron interests of the family.[10] He appears to have been an inventor of some originality; his invention of the rifled steel cannon brought him international decorations and a greater family fortune. Newspapers remembered that Francis Henry had been received by Queen Victoria and that during " 'a famine in the Canary Islands he sent a free cargo of wheat and was made by the king of Portugal the heredity Marquis di Casa Bisa, a title he never used'."[11] The style of newspaper reporting had obviously changed greatly since his father's day, for Francis Henry's notices are bare and personally unrevealing. Certainly, no matter what the reporting style, the tireless need to organize, to accumulate, and to complicate that his father and Edgar's grandfather demonstrated would be hard for anyone to match.

Not having known his paternal grandfather was an absence that could doubtless be sustained; but the vivid presence of an older half-brother could not so easily be tolerated. For Edgar was not only a second son but a half-brother to the favored son who had received the by-now traditional family first name of Francis. Francis Saltus Saltus (1849-1889) was born to his father's first wife, Julia Augusta Hubbard (1829-1850), a mere twenty-one when she died. The family seems to have divided into two halves: the two "Franks" made a pair; Edgar and his mother, Eliza Howe Evertson, made another. The family separation into two camps is even reflected in the children's names: Francis Saltus was named for his father and paternal grandfather; Edgar Evertson for his maternal grandfather. The family middle names compound the symbolic separation. Frank was his father's boy; Edgar, his mother's.

Even more interesting psychologically and socially is the fact that in this generation the business energy transmitted so powerfully from Solomon to Francis to Francis Henry broke down completely. Both Francis and Edgar were devoted to literature. The literary bond may have drawn the half-brothers together while the politics of the family pulled them apart. The parents, as they frequently do, probably used their children to displace their own marital tensions. We can only surmise the particulars of the "ceaseless conflict between his parents" of which Edgar was the "battleground."[12] It remained domestic until he was seven; thereafter, his parents apparently separated permanently.

While the father took Frank abroad with him, Edgar was enrolled in and completed his preparatory school training at St. Paul's in Concord, New Hampshire, one of the country's upper-class training schools. After two fall terms at Yale, in 1872 and 1873, which he completed without distinction, Edgar went abroad with his mother.[13] By this time, according to Marie Giles, Edgar, as "the pampered only child of an adoring mother," had become "selfish and self-centered.[14]

Edgar probably acquired a good deal of his intellectual and personal fire during these years abroad, which may have lasted until 1878, when he entered Columbia Law School, because his mother felt "that he must have some kind of an occupation." Between 1873 and 1878 he studied at the Sorbonne and in Heidelberg and Munich. France was to become his "patrie psychique" as it was to other contemporaries: to his own brother, to James Huneker, and to Stuart Merrill. Merrill, whose poetry in French remains a respectable part of modern French poetic history although he is virtually unknown in America, introduced Saltus to Victor Hugo. Saltus also met Leconte de Lisle and Paul Verlaine, writers closer to his generation than the Romantic Hugo who still so powerfully dominated French literature.

In Germany, Arthur Schopenhauer became to Saltus "daily food," and his two works on pessimism amply testify to the diet. In England, he met Oşcar Wilde, Owen Meredith, Baron Harden-Hickey, and others. Thus between the ages of eighteen and twenty-three Edgar assimilated the major influences of his career from which he developed a style and a point of view. His version of style he pieced and knit from French and English examples; his version of philosophic pessimism he derived from Schopenhauer and Eduard von Hartmann.

Although Edgar received his law degree in 1880, he was probably not expected to practice. More likely he needed merely to acquire a respectable education, his mother's wish for an occupation notwithstanding.[15] Frank, the brilliant, irresistible elder brother encouraged Edgar to write; and this Edgar presumably did. He also fell in love, as his third wife says he so frequently did. When he married Helen Sturgis Read, the daughter of a J. P. Morgan partner, at Grace Episcopal Church in 1883, his first book, *Balzac,* was soon to appear. He seemed indeed to have done well in solidifying the twin bases of human achievement and happiness—love and work.

The best and perhaps the only description we have of Edgar as he was in the 1880's we owe to James Huneker. The sketch acquires greater force because of its contrast with Frank, whom Huneker also knew. Frank, whose Apollonian looks "were historical" when Huneker met him, usually arrived at Moulds' Cafe "about noon and wrote and talked till the last trump, which was at two a.m.; sometimes later. The classic type of Bohemianism that has quite vanished.[16] Huneker ranks the eloquence of Frank's discourse second only to Oscar Wilde's—high praise from another great talker whose own conversation staggered H. L. Mencken.[17]

The letters Frank wrote to Brander Matthews between 1877 and 1881 bubble not only with talk about poetry and music but with inserted poems as well.[18] He is credited with a knowledge not of five or eight but of thirteen languages. If he was the "perfect Bohemian" Huneker thought him, the perfect bohemian may be the imperfect artist.

Edgar has not left so bohemian a reputation although he, his brother, and James Huneker share a legendary love for the ladies. Perhaps Edgar's father's strength and his brother's genius combined, as Marie Giles suggests, to make him feel inadequate. Although she also suggests that the consequences of dissipation were so hammered at him by his mother that he completed his law training, her lectures did not make him practice law or keep him from the "balls, receptions, and festivities" common to a young man of his class. The New York Social Register for the period shows his summer residence, predictably, at Narragansett Pier, just across from Newport, Rhode Island. To the delights of society (his writings show he did not always consider them delights), the "brilliant" Edgar brought a handsomeness different from his brother's; for Edgar was "dark, Italian, petit-maître, a prosemaster and a philosopher."[19]

Marie Giles never knew the Edgar Saltus of these early, presumably buoyant years. It seems unlikely that Edgar had already developed his "almost physical disability to tell the truth, if that truth were disagreeable."[20] According to Mrs. Saltus, Edgar's evasion of the unpleasant was as marked a personal characteristic as his attraction to women; he reputedly sustained multiple love affairs tthroughout his life. These characteristics may have left him time to write thirteen books (six novels, one collection of short stories, four nonfiction works, two editing and translating jobs) in the eight years between his marriage and his divorce (1883-1891), but we may be permitted some skepticism. The evidence is insufficient to assume in Saltus a temperament as gargantuan as Huneker's.[21]

The failure of his first marriage aroused an intense bitterness in Saltus. In his fictionalized version of the break-up, recorded in *Madam Sapphira* (1893), Saltus puts the blame entirely on the wife who coldly engineers two compromising situations with the husband so that she may be free to marry her lover. The husband is faithful and faultless; the wife, faithless and unprincipled. The facts show, however, that Saltus married one of the named co-respondents, Elsie Welsh Smith in London in 1894.[22] Helen married William Oothout in 1892, only a year later. The latter's name, as improbable a one as any Saltus ever coined, marks him as the original of Ablaut, the lover in *Madam Sapphira*. The virulence of Saltus' attack in his novel on his first wife seems out of character in a patrician New Yorker presumably highly trained in the qualities of restraint and decorum.

The 1890's did not, therefore, begin gaily for Edgar Saltus. His personal difficulties were compounded by scandalous newspaper reports about his divorce proceedings. Like his fictional counterpart, Carol Nevius, in *Madam Sapphira*, Saltus was in Europe when the shockingly detailed newspaper articles appeared. Like him, he also finally succeeded in having the names of the two co-respondents deleted from the divorce action. The newspapers again carried headlines: "NO DIVORCE SUIT FOR NOVELIST SALTUS; HIS WIFE WITHDRAWS HER SENSATIONAL CHARGES AGAINST THE EXPONENT OF EROTIC LITERATURE; CO-RESPONDENTS EXONERATED.[23] Indeed, the headline suggests that the Saltus reputation may be a second-hand one, derived from the garbled, grotesque newspaper view of him. Perhaps the distortions of the newspapers were simply adopted by other critics; but there is no perhaps about the fact that ostracism accompanied divorce in 1891.[24]

II *A Counter-legend*

On the basis of what we know about Saltus and his environment we can construct a counter-legend to Sadakichi Hartmann's. We can imagine the young man exposed to the New York City of the 1880's when he was not away for the summer or in Europe. The city had survived its Civil War draft riots (Edgar might remember them if his family had remained in town that July, 1863), the panic and depression of the 1870's, the stock-fraud scandals, and the municipal corruption exploded by Thomas Nast's anti-Tammany cartoons. Saltus grew up and lived, therefore, amid dichotomy and extraordinary material changes. Booms went with busts; spectacular economic and industrial expansion accompanied recessions and violent strikes, riots, corruption.

In New York, older families like the Brevoorts, the Schermerhorns, the Rhinelanders remained in the Washington Square area while the newer wealthy—the Rockefellers, the Vanderbilts—and the more enterprising older families followed the city in its restless thrust northwards. What was "uptown" when Saltus was a boy had long been considered "downtown" by the time he died. The center of fashion and wealth was moving to Madison Square and even as far as 42nd Street and eventually to the part of Fifth Avenue that bordered Central Park.

There were pleasures—for the young man-about-town doubtless formed a part of the Central Park promenades and carriage parades. He may have attended band concerts in the park which was one of the few public places where rich and poor mingled in a social intercourse more acceptable than that which occurred in the gambling halls and brothels of the Five Points and the Tenderloin slum districts. He doubtless had his own carriage, and he may have joined other riders on the bridle paths which were part of Frederick Law Olmsted's original plans for the park.

Olmsted managed to acquire against substantial opposition the huge tract of land which makes up Central Park—a feat he probably could not have managed in the 1880's against the will of the city's more powerful financial powers whom Saltus was so frequently to satirize. Indeed, mammoth new structures rather than public parks characterized the 1880's. The Metropolitan Museum of Art opened at its current site in 1880; and in 1883 both the Brooklyn Bridge and the Metropolitan Opera House were completed. The former is still a magnificent wedding of design and engineering, the latter an architectural horror, built only to accommodate the Wall Street families who could not get a box in the Academy of Music downtown, very near the Moulds' Cafe where Huneker drank with Frank Saltus. In this round of the social war between the old and the new rich, Saltus could see "culture," art and music, become pawns in the game of conspicuous consumption.

New York was growing horizontally toward the farms of Harlem and vertically with buildings eight, fifteen, twenty, and even more stories high. The great waves of immigrants from central and southern Europe who crowded the already dense slum areas helped to build the skyscrapers and new elevated railways that carried them to work. It was already a jest that one could hear more English spoken in Paris that in many parts of New York.

When Saltus spoke later in life of these great changes, he had become nostalgic for the imagined sufficiency of the past. As a young man he quite likely enjoyed, as Huneker did, the great variety of cultures the city contained. But Saltus was very rarely to use realistic details of place, manners, and occupations with analytic intent in his novels. When he offers such details, they are decorative rather than explanatory or exploratory. In a writer who has left practically no direct self-examination and remarkably little probing of others, fictional or living, it is perhaps more than usually tempting to rely on external description in the hope that context can suggest what the man cannot or will not divulge.

III *Death, Divorce and Decline*

Marie Saltus describes the Edgar of the 1880's as turning "out novels like flapjacks [and] entertaining his acquaintances in the intervals." But several pages later we are told "he never wrote a book less than three times," remaining in his art "on his knees before the spirit of Flaubert."[25] Marie's words suggest both the flippancy and the seriousness that may well have characterized Edgar's public and artistic selves.

The two ascertainable personal disasters of the 1880's—the divorce from Helen Read and the untimely death of his brother Frank—did not diminish his productivity. Furthermore, Edgar's involvement with the philosophy of pessimism pre-dates these events. Something less definable and even more pervasive than the experiences of death and divorce made Edgar receptive to Schopenhauer: some basic dissatisfaction with or implicit rebellion against himself and his place that even he could not define too clearly. Oddly enough, the experience of death and divorce did not change or deepen Edgar's work unless we risk the judgment that they did affect and make possible what most critics consider the apogee of his career, *Imperial Purple*, which he completed on November 1, 1891, in Paris and which he probably began just after his divorce decree was declared final on June 18 of that year.

The death of Francis did deeply affect his father, who was still using black-bordered stationary in April, 1891, and expressing his great grief and great desire to publish his son's manuscripts;

he undertook, in fact, an edition of Frank's works at a reputed cost of thirty thousand dollars.[26] He speaks with great affection of his charming and gifted son whose obituary in *Time* conjures up an improvisatory genius, "witty, audacious," and thoroughly irrepressible: "He left enough verse to fill twelve volumes, besides the music and librettos of seven operas, four of which are comic and one grand."[27] What survives is not the work but the personality of a prodigy who wrote poetry and music too easily in a Victorian poetic diction and with a rhythm too conventional and smooth to outlive the poet's own life.

Edgar has left as his only public response to his brother several paragraphs in a reminiscence of writers he had known. His remarks make his brother one of a group of poets Saltus knew; others were Edgar Fawcett, Owen Meredith, Stuart Merrill. All were facile, none achieved greatness; and Saltus recognized that their hold on posterity was fragile. He adds one more characteristic anecdote to the Frank Saltus personal legend: "On one occasion, in less than an hour, Francis Saltus scribbled a ballad to Patti in four languages and put it to music. His facility was frightful and, as he never revised, it was fatal." "Like Fawcett," he adds, "he too missed it."[28]

The death of his mother and strong indications of creative decline occurred during the 1890's when Saltus began his voluminous journalistic writing for newspapers and magazines and even signed contracts for the "scissors and paste" books of which his letters to Van Vechten show him to be much ashamed.[29] Moreover, new marital problems awaited him. His marriage to Elsie Welsh Smith in 1894 brought him only brief domestic happiness; for, before his daughter Elsie was born in 1897, he and his wife were already estranged. In a private notebook Edgar recorded his distress over the separate lives he and Elsie had begun to live even while they were together. In 1901 the second Mrs. Saltus obtained a legal separation and successfully blocked, until her death in Paris in 1909, every effort of Edgar to obtain a divorce. That she so strongly refused to accede to a divorce suggests a resentment whose origins we can only surmise. She also successfully halted Edgar's efforts to gain custody of their child who seems to have had to appear in court more than once when she was three and four years old.

According to newspaper accounts, Mrs. Saltus left her husband in April, 1900, because of his heavy drinking and cruel treatment; the *Tribune* of February 15, 1902, reports his countercontention "that his mode of life is entirely studious and his habits strictly ascetic."[30] These proceedings are reported more briefly and more perfunctorily than his divorce, indicating either that Saltus had lost by 1901 much of his newsworthiness or that other personal scandals were juicier.

Somewhere around the turn of the century (Marie's biography frequently omits dates), Edgar saw Marie Giles through a window that looked out on Narragansett Pier. He was a successful writer, the more attractive for his reputed wickedness; she was a youthful, aspiring writer "more pampered and self-willed than himself" and perhaps therefore the better able to manage him.[31] For the remainder of her biography has as its true subject Marie's management of a gifted, difficult, and ultimately physically suffering man. Their life before and after their marriage in 1911 is difficult to piece together. Edgar appears to have moved in with Marie and her invalid mother and aunt on a platonic basis some time before their marriage, and he apparently followed her to Europe and to California. Although there were times after their marriage when they lived apart, their brief separations were not due to Saltus' *don juanisme*, which seems to have dwindled into teas and epistolary exchanges with younger ladies.

Mrs. Saltus herself accepts 1912 as the end of her husband's creative life. His productivity had greatly decreased; in ten years he had published two novels (one more was posthumously published, another was never completed); some privately printed essays; and *Imperial Orgy*, a hysterical counterpart to *Imperial Purple*. During this period he also wrote newspaper articles predictably expressing intense anti-Hun sentiments and indicating his strong belief that "anything antebellum has been, is now, and ever will be prehistoric."[32]

IV *The Ironist's Dilemma*

Perhaps the best demonstration of the zest, whimsy, and exaggeration that were part of the earlier Edgar is a letter that deserves full quotation as the almost single direct autobiographical statement by Saltus himself. The fundamental distance he maintains is part of the persona of the ironist; he adds to rather than detracts from his rakish public image. He quite thoroughly enjoys his creation:

> It is delightful for you to ask me so many interesting questions. You give me an opportunity of talking of myself. There is nothing that I enjoy more. In that, however, I can hardly call myself unique. We are all the same.
>
> To begin, then, at the beginning, I was born in this city, in the house which I now occupy, thirty-five years ago. My mother did me the honor of being a direct descendant of Rip Van Dam, and from my father, I received the name of the Roman family to which his progenitors belonged.
>
> My infancy is vague, my adolescence remote. The earliest event that I definitely recall is the composition of a sonnet. There were some more events of the same character, until I discovered that prose is more difficult than verse. I tried to form a style of my own in the writing of love letters, and, failing, attacked the biography of Balzac. It was my first fruit, and being utterly detestable, was widely praised. This occurred nine years ago. Success made me melancholy, and in a wedding tour which I then undertook I wrote *The Philosophy of Disenchantment,* which is, I think, the gloomiest and worst book ever published. Out of sheer laziness, I then produced a history of atheism, *The Anatomy of Negation,* which has been honoured by international dislike. Need I state that of all my children it is the one that I prefer? After that I entered the drawing-room of fiction with Mr. Incoul and left it three years ago with *The Pace That Kills.* Since then I may fairly claim to be haunted by antiquity. If I was not at the siege of Troy, no one will convince me that I did not ride in wide chariots over the white roads of Greece, that I did not eat the clitoris of tigresses with Caligula, and assist with Heliogabalus at the wedding of the Sun and the Moon. There was an hour when I hoped to be known as a novelist; I hope now to make at least a pencil-mark in history. To my thinking, of all pursuits it is the most aristocratic. But on that subject I may change my mind, indeed I am sure I shall consistency is a confession of failure. It is the faithless, not the faithful, who know the enjoyments of life. They are never bored. My own hours of boredom have been few. My existence, it is true, has been passed in libraries where my adventures have been with phrases and my escapades with lexicons; but such as it is, it has brought me a great variety of disbeliefs, no less, in fact, than three hundred and sixty-five, one for every day in the calendar, leaving one, on leap year, for twenty-four hours the privilege of

neither believing nor disbelieving, and generally confirming an opinion I hold, that educated man should not have a prejudice to his name.

Edgar Saltus, Bourgeoisophobus[33]

This earlier Saltus never entirely disappeared. In later life, he reserved his greater directness and warmth for persons closer to him. His warmest extant letters are to Van Vechten, whom he affectionately addresses as "Dear Genius" and "Dear Interpreter"; to Huneker, usually "Dear Merlin" or "Cher Maître"; and to his daughter who is "Carissima." When Huneker and Van Vechten evinced interest in his works, he responded lavishly. He answered fully and generously Van Vechten's detailed questions about the publishing history of many works (Van Vechten must have been preparing his essay on Saltus which appeared in *The Merry Go Round* in 1918).

Saltus' humor was unfailing, even after his return from the hospital after what might have been a bout with the nephritis (or Bright's disease) which, with its classic corollaries, pulmonary edema and an enlarged heart, eventually killed him. After his return home, he says, "I have been entertaining that inertia which death, in revenge I suppose, puts on those for whom it has come and not got. We live on lies."[34] But his "amazed appreciation" of another writer's interests in him overcame his post-hospital inertia, resulting in his most interesting extant set of letters and ultimately in a meeting with his admirer, Carl Van Vechten.

The cheer, warmth and humor of these letters co-exist with Edgar's sense of his literary isolation and his final pitiless self-estimate. When, in one of his letters to Van Vechten, Saltus writes, "In earlier days I tried to whip myself up to her," to the true muse, he suggests his own abdication from that rare effort in art he so admired; for Edgar Saltus had by 1918 and 1919 "missed it"—and he knew it.[35]

He had also missed the "health and indifference" he considered crucial to contentment.[36] By the time he had finished *The Imperial Orgy* in 1920, his legs were so bad it took him ten minutes to walk the few yards from the Arizona Apartments at 508 West 114th Street (today a Columbia University dormitory) to the corner of Amsterdam Avenue. After a terminal illness of eight days, he died in his apartment on July 31, 1921. His ashes were placed in the new Saltus vault at Sleepy Hollow Cemetery in Tarrytown; for his father had removed the family dead from their original vault in Marble Cemetery on Second Street in Manhattan. The site was new, but its legendary associations were as old as Washington Irving's tale about it. Its strong local color suited the old local Saltus family that had to some degree reflected the growth pattern of a nation and a class in its development from sea captains to sonneteers. The last surviving male in this particular branch of the Saltus family had long ceased to echo, if ever he had echoed, the wish of his grandfather "to be placed in difficulties that he might have the opportunity to extricate himself."

The grandfather was speaking of circumstantial difficulties attendant upon a life of mercantile pursuits. The grandson, spared on the whole the necessity for accumulating money, could turn to letters. Perhaps he arrived too late. Perhaps the Eastern Dutch-English strain, so long the provider of the nation's literature, had given out. (Melville and Whitman were probably the last vigorous representatives of the old stock.) Perhaps Edgar's painless shift from the Dutch church of his forefathers to Episcopalianism suggests the more social character of religion in his class and in his day and a consequently more attenuated sense of identity and purpose.

The indigenous Saltus may, of course, present as many difficulties as the exotic Saltus. Both constructions of Saltus must be fragmentary since they rest on relatively little concrete evidence. Perhaps both come together in Saltus' posture as ironist. The ironist saw the limitations of his environment—New York and America—and tried to rouse it and educate it. The posture of irony was well-chosen, but it was unfortunately undercut by Saltus' need to please.

When Saltus spoke of theosophy as a school of good manners, he was reinforcing earlier comments which suggest a strong respect for whatever attitudes, acts, and manners would lessen friction in human intercourse. An extension of this attitude occasionally leads to a point of view more naturalist than resigned, but the reverse is more often true. For example, "Whatever we learn," he writes in a private notebook, "we learn too late, sometimes too soon, never when we should—Whichever way we turn, we are sure of nothing but regret. The one safe course, if there be one, is to close the eyes, fold the hands and await the will of the gods—we are ruled, not rulers, and I fancy none of us have the pretension to change the course of events."[37] The side of himself that speaks of drift and fatality objectified itself in pleasing. Edgar pleased the ladies, and he eventually gave the public the image of the artist it wanted—and thereby lost his own way.

Yet no one knew better than Saltus the dangers of pleasing: "Try to please, said Epictetus, and you are lost." His own version of Epictetus' warning was especially strong: "To obstinacy, everything yields. The point is to be obstinate." If this obstinacy refers to the conduct of the artist and to his artistic practice, as it must, then to be obstinate in the Brown Decades was the only route to artistic and personal integrity. Such obstinacy is not indifference but a form of challenge and combat.

Saltus wanted to please and he wanted to be obstinate, and he was finally unable to turn these opposing desires into a source of artistic strength. He knew that the price of obstinacy might be frightening: "The little boy in a high chair who draws the picture of an ogre so hideous that though it is his own creation he screams with fright. Do we not all of us resemble that little boy." He moved only tentatively toward confrontations with the ogres of his own creation, but it is to his credit that he knew they existed. He apparently could not harmonize the sociality his whole life had trained him for with the rigor his art demanded of him—a conflict reminiscent of that of a better writer, F. Scott Fitzgerald. Although Saltus was born inside the class Fitzgerald felt alien to, he had enough of the outsider's vision to see that his golden girls and lads were destined for destruction.

Sometimes Saltus' catalogues recall Fitzgerald's in *The Crack-Up*. In a catalogue of titles, none of which he ever used, Saltus includes Kisses and Crusts, Fast and Loose, Scaffolds and Altars, Sweet and Twenty, In Silk and Scarlet. Like Fitzgerald, Saltus was obsessed by the magic of love, of youth, of money. If the legend of his devastating personal attraction is true, then he overexpended himself in that persona for little gratification and at great cost to his art. The happiness he always said was an illusion was obviously one he believed in—his protests to the contrary. And when, caught in his own grim mirror, he saw the ogre of discrepancy between desire and achievement, so characteristic of the Romantic temperament, he seems to have covered the mirror, folded his hands, and awaited the will of the gods.

CHAPTER 2

"I Am, Therefore I Suffer"[1]

Le Chrétien est impie en Asie, le musulman en Europe, le papiste à Londres, le calviniste à Paris. Qu'est-ce donc qu'un impie? Tout le monde l'est-il ou personne.

Diderot, copied into
Saltus notebook, c. 1890.

. . . the cardinal, uncontrovertible tenet that life is a burden will remain firm and changeless to the end of time.

The Philosophy of Disenchantment

OTHER AMERICAN WRITERS of the years Van Wyck Brooks called "confident" (1885-1915) testified with Saltus to blasted promise and sensed impending disaster, personal or social or both. In the later work of Whitman and Melville, as well as in that of younger writers like Mark Twain, Henry James, Henry Adams and Ambrose Bierce, the criticism of prevailing values has an edge, often of futility, that was non-existent in ante-bellum critics like Emerson and Thoreau. The criticism of Emerson and Thoreau against the false power of "things," strong as it is, diminishes not by a shaving their remarkably buoyant sense of personal possibility and power. Within the era labelled "confident" or "optimistic," enough writers and thinkers were unconfident and pessimistic to suggest in little a picture similar to that of the 1920's. Within the later decade, against the public picture of prosperity, flamboyant and presumably persuasive to the majority, is the private picture of national failure portrayed by writers like Brooks, Mencken, Pound, and others.

How strong the intellectual discontent between 1880 and 1915 was has yet to be fully measured. Even if we judge it weak, sufficient discontent existed to modify the solid picture of complacency and imperception that the generation of Mencken and Brooks projected in order to destroy it. Many talented men left the United States never to return. The number of expatriates is instructive; Henry James, Whistler, Henry Harland, Stuart Merrill, Francis Viélé-Griffin were among them. (Very few traveled in the reverse direction; Richard Le Gallienne was one.) Saltus himself wandered restlessly and frequently between the United States and Europe.

To the larger intellectual discontent of the period, the historian of ideas must add the Saltusian formulation of pessimism—one contained in two books and one essay. These works have a surer, if minor, place in American social and intellectual history than they have been given. In *The Philosophy of Disenchantment* (1885), *The Anatomy of Negation* (1886), and "What Pessimism is Not," Saltus stirred a post-war generation not yet situated in the robust imperialism and Naturalism more characteristic of the last decade of the nineteenth century.

I The Philosphy of Disenchantment

The term "pessimism" has some tight philosophic core, as the term "Romantic" has some precise historical critical core. For Western philosophy, pessimism is traditionally regarded as that doctrine formulated by Arthur Schopenhauer against the classic formulation of optimism by Gottfried von Leibniz and English Deism. Schopenhauer's formulation rests powerfully and consciously upon an older pessimism—Buddhism. As Saltus himself put it, the modern pessimist is "a Buddhist strayed from the Orient."[2] Since pessimism begins with the axiom that life is fundamentally evil, the root problem for both Eastern and Western pessimist is individual existence; when it disappears, sorrow will disappear. Saltus shows himself aware of the somewhat tighter, more technical meaning of pessimism in his accurate, clear, and reasonably thorough examination of the life and doctrine of Schopenhauer and Eduard von Hartmann in *The Philosophy of Disenchantment.* He locates Schopenhauer in the history of philosophy, in his point in time after Immanuel Kant, indicating his reestablishment of the *Ding an Sich* as Will, and his opposition to his "transcendental" contemporaries, Johann Fichte and Georg Hegel.

That Saltus felt himself a pioneer, a vanguard proponent of a new religion not yet fully defined (and therefore so much the more attractive) deserves underlining. Although Mencken considered pessimism already old-fashioned by the time Saltus wrote about it, the evidence suggests otherwise. *The World as Will and Idea,* published in 1819, had a delayed vogue. Schopenhauer's popularity in Germany and elsewhere begins in the 1850's. The article generally considered to have introduced him to the English-speaking public appeared in 1853 and the translation of *The World as Will and Idea* (1884-1886), his major work, was not yet complete when Saltus published *The Philosophy of Disenchantment* in 1885.[3] Von Hartmann's *Philosophie des Unbewissten,* published in 1869, appeared in English in 1886, a year after the Saltus work. That von Hartmann's ideas were a center of controversy on the Continent for a quarter of a century deserves recording and that the views of Schopenhauer, the high priest of pessimism, and of his student, von Hartmann, had not permeated beyond a specialist's circle seems clear. Indeed, a better case might be made that Saltus was accepting or encouraging a point of view just becoming known. Mencken's own championship of Nietzsche was neither more nor less *au courant* than Saltus' of Schopenhauer.[4]

After a first chapter which ranges through religions and literatures with an ease to make the specialist of today flinch, Saltus boldly concludes that "life to the Christian is a problem, to the Brahmin a burden, to the Buddhist a dream, and to the pessimist a nightmare."[5] When he is moved to an unexpected peroration on Giacomo Leopardi as a disenchanted poet, Saltus exposes his literary bias to which he returns in the final chapter. In the modernists of his day—in Henry James, Emile Zola, the brothers Goncourt, Stendhal, Gustave Flaubert, Ivan Turgenev, Charles Baudelaire, and Edgar Allan Poe—he finds melancholy support of the pessimistic tenet that "life is an affliction."

The man in search of relief from the affliction of life and its attendant illusions of love and happiness may find it, Schopenhauer suggests, in art and contemplation, or in the more rigorous solutions of asceticism or absolute chastity. Suicide will not do because it merely destroys individual existence, leaving the species intact and the problem of existence unsolved. Although Saltus accepts his mentor on the futility of suicide, he considers asceticism and chastity somewhat eccentric forms of liberation from life. He turns Schopenhauer's acutely misanthropic doctrines into a more reasonable, more compassionate code of behavior that includes solitude conducive to thought and creation —solitude like Emerson's, like Thoreau's (the examples are Saltus'); avoidance of superficial society; an awareness of interior as against exterior values; and the development of self as against the accumulation of wealth. These values are clearly counter to those of the Gilded Age and its leaders. Twain named the age, and Saltus echoes Twain when he calls the era's élite the "Gilded Gang."

After his discussion of Schopenhauer, Saltus turns to Eduard von Hartmann (1842-1906), whom he had interviewed in Berlin and who was then the most famous of Schopenhauer's disciples and is still referred to in psychoanalytic textbooks as a pre-Freudian because of his conception of the Unconscious.[6] Von Hartmann's doctrine allowed for a mitigated pessimism which the example of his life supported, surrounded as he was by wife and children in contrast to Schopenhauer's misogynistic, solitary personal life. As Saltus put it: "He endeavors in everyday life to prove the practical value of evolutionary pessimism, which it is his wish to substitute for the indifferentism and quietist doctrines of Schopenhauer."[7] Von Hartmann's Absolute is not the irrational Will but the Unconscious—more properly a metaphysical, a cosmic, than a psychological principle.

In contrast to his teacher, von Hartmann urges that man is "most happy when he is the unconscious dupe of his illusions."[8] The Unconscious, therefore, permits illusion and the consequent individual mitigation of misery. Von Hartmann also uses the concept of the Unconscious to support his belief that the universe is evolving toward redemption from evil. Thus, he both has and has not Schopenhauer's Will, keeping it but making it unconscious and directive instead of irrational.

Saltus must have found in his pessimists corroboration of social criticisms he himself had made. Although not yet noted for his wit, he must have vibrated sympathetically to Schopenhauer's contention that society does not appreciate it. He probably agreed that intelligence makes a man an outcast in a society that values mediocrity. If "society is a mill of the conventional which grinds individualities into a tiresome sameness of sample," then "to please in society . . . one needs to be scatterbrained or ignorant."[9]

He steps out of his middleman role to proclaim in his own voice that "Progress is as undeniably the chimera of the present century as the resurrection of the dead was that of the tenth."[10] To call progress a delusion required some courage. About politics, however, Saltus is casual, erratic, even commonplace. He cites Socialist opposition as the strongest foe pessimism has because its doctrine is so centrally based on future material good. Other political references in this second published Saltus work are few and naïvely conservative as they are not in his later journalistic writings. In *The Philosophy of Disenchantment* Saltus regards the New York draft riots and the Paris Commune as threats to law and order which call for conventional suppression. Yet his evocation of current social horrors—the factory, the slum, the prison—is vivid, though perfunctory. He is not, however, moved by any special social doctrine as other figures associated with the esthetic 1890's were; Stuart Merrill, Oscar Wilde, and Frank Harris were all attracted to Socialist doctrine.

In his concluding chapter Saltus defers to the assumed conservatism of his readers, assuring them that elimination of happiness in the after-life is "no atheism, though the arguments that follow may seem to savor of the agnostic." He makes his position even easier for the orthodox Christian to understand, possibly to accept, when he clarifies: pessimism "does not in its ethics differ in any respect from the sublime teachings of the Christian faith." He also assures his readers that the individual's aspiration for liberation does not acquit him "of any of the obligations that he owes to society."[11] These demurrers need not excessively dilute the special content of pessimism; other strongly antitheist philosophies have not dissociated themselves from the Christian ethos. (Socialism is one example.) Moreover, the total effect of the work is not a diluted one.

When Saltus says few men have "the courage to acknowledge that they are miserable," we remember Thoreau's "the mass of men lead lives of quiet desperation" and we know the aware pessimist is thinking of and addressing his unaware, Anglo-Saxon (the term is his) common reader whose common faith is custom and for whom it is "bad form to question the value of life."[12] Saltus may have erred in presenting scientific pessimism to that reader. He certainly erred in his assumption that scientific pessimism (the term, rarely used by the two German propagators of the doctrine, probably derives from James Sully) would be his or anyone else's religion. Unlike agnosticism, it did not become a recognizable movement or acquire an apostle with the dedication and force of "the great agnostic," Robert Ingersoll, who influenced at least two of Saltus' friends, Edgar Fawcett and Stuart Merrill.[13] Saltus had presumably decided against a sharper commitment to agnosticism. His next book deepens his ambivalent stance toward himself and his public.

We are left, nevertheless, with an energetic, vivacious presentation of a melancholy, apparently resigned doctrine, a surface paradox not uncommon in the history of human thought. To that paradox we owe Saltus' most effective expositional work, the one most deserving of James Gibbons Huneker's remarkable compliment: "What writer, with the exception of William James, can make such daring and conclusive expositions of philosophy as Mr. Saltus? We must go to France for his counterpart."[14]

II The Anatomy of Negation

In *The Anatomy of Negation* (1886) Saltus continues his work as an apostle and popularizer. His previous book had examined the modern version of scientific or theoretic pessimism; this one ambitiously traces the "tableau of anti-theism from Kapila to Leconte de Lisle."[15] He finds that anti-theism, a relative of skepticism and pessimism, has had for its champions schools and thinkers from the ancient and modern world. Some moderns, like Pierre Maupertius, Baron d'Holbach, and Jacques-André Naigeon, are not so well known to the general reader today; nor are the simplest tenets of Eastern thinkers. Saltus once more shows himself widely cultivated, an excellent middleman; but he is already attempting impossible encyclopedic coverage.

The chapter on Christianity, for example, extremely interesting and primarily concerned with the historical Jesus, also covers the history of the early and medieval church, its heretics (gnostics, iconoclasts, Albigensians, etc.), the Inquisition, the Reformation, Erasmus, Rabelais, Montaigne, Galileo and so forth, Such coverage suggests the textbook to a contemporary reader. Although fashion accounts for some of our dissatisfaction with his approach, a book with a thesis so bold and so boldly announced ought to have been more selective and thereby more thorough. Moreover, in his prefatory note, Saltus unfortunately exposes his own ambivalence before the common reader he at once fears and courts: "To avoid misconception, it may be added that no attempt has been made to prove anything." With this book and this assertion he undercuts the center of his work and, as Eric McKitrick puts it, "bade an early farewell to anything resembling formal polemic."[16]

The text is, happily, stronger than the prefatory demurrer suggests. Saltus manages to fit Jesus into a history of anti-theism: "He was the most entrancing of nihilists, but he was not an innovator," for he built upon Essene doctrine. Saltus warns us that Essene doctrine makes thorough sense only if we realize that it was preparing men for death, not life. The imminent end of the world underlines, perhaps explains, Christ's emphasis on renunciation of self, on voluntary poverty, on communal property, and on the celibate life. Saltus believes, moreover, that only the exoteric Christian doctrine has come down to us. The esoteric and pessimistic doctrine may have been that life is evil and subsists through procreation: "ergo, abolish procreation and the evil disappears."[17]

In the remainder of the work Saltus picks out iconoclasts like Montaigne, Spinoza, Voltaire, d'Holbach, and the German idealists and generally equates orthodoxy with intolerance and dissent with tolerance: "as skepticism arose intolerance declined." He dances away from the new Positivist movement as more properly relativist: "for positivism, if positive at all, is positive that there is nothing positive." In his last chapter, "A Poet's Verdict," Baudelaire and the Parnassians emerge as artistic parallels to philosophic doubt. In Leconte de Lisle, particularly, an anti-theist before Schopenhauer, we close the circle begun with Kapila, a predecessor of Buddha. Saltus' support of de Lisle's conception of Christianity as "an artistic creation, powerfully conceived, venerable in its antiquity, and one whose place is now marked in the museum of history" is implicit.[18]

Besides the misanthropy of the later Mark Twain, Saltus' exposition of the essential absurdity of existence sometimes resembles the average student term paper: objective, deferential, unwilling to upset the professor (in this case, the American audience). Occasionally, he surprises his reader and surfaces his criticism of false values. Sometimes he reveals his own sense of having been born into a wrong society. Occasionally he more than merits the comments of contemporary reviewers about one or the other of his two books on pessimism: "audacious, defiant, scornful, despairing"; "it flashes and stings and fascinates." On other occasions he merits Julian Hawthorne's undiluted barbs: "But this is a book of nothing; of phrases; of anecdotes; of Lilliputian impertinences."[19]

There are, as James Sully (1842-1923) so charmingly phrased it, "permanent elements of utility in pessimism."[20] Its temporary "elements of utility" are more pertinent here, though not necessarily easier to identify than its permanent elements. The central temporary or local utility of presenting life, as Schopenhauer has it, as "a path of redhot coals with a few cool places here and there" is corrective. Historically, Schopenhauer's pessimism is a valuable corrective to rationalism. Saltus' pessimism is a corrective to the values of Washington Square and Wall Street and, by extension, of the United States in the 1880's.

Schopenhauer has frequently been attacked for his political conservatism and for his essentially non-philosophical doctrines. The attacks are valid, but they do not tell us enough. Thomas Mann, well aware of Schopenhauer's anti-humanist elements, nonetheless considered his corrective role still important in 1939. In an introduction to selections from Schopenhauer's works, Mann presents as his central reassertion, "the idea of connection between pessimism and humanism." The great paradox of Schopenhauer's legacy is that it is precisely in his "derogation of the one-time godlike reason" that his humaneness shows. He "lifts men out of the biological sphere of nature, makes his own feeling and understanding soul the theatre where the will meets its reverses, and sees in the human being the savior of all creation."[21] Schopenhauer's thought is not a glorification of that instinct become malice which Mann considered the ruling nightmare of the first third of the twentieth century.

When Saltus refers to Baudelaire in *The Philosophy of Disenchantment* as "the poet of boredom," and when he speaks of our fear of boredom, of our need to "kill time, . . . to escape ennui," of pessimism as come "to deliver us from boredom," of modern life as provoking a dreadful "universal nausea," an "immense nausea," we are not merely listening to an already tired esthete.[22] The terms "boredom" and "nausea" may today suggest greater content than they did to a previous generation. Pessimism, by its questioning of the total sufficiency of reason and by its insistence on discontinuity in evolution and progress, is one ancestor of Existentialism—of a twentieth century sometimes merely glib about its awareness of the irrational in man, about its experience of throwbacks, of visible rents in the evolutionary tissue that seemed so whole to so many in Saltus' time.

What the pessimist calls "pain" the existentialist calls "anguish." Beneath the terms "boredom," "nausea," "pain" is a sharp criticism of the acquisitive instinct and a sharp sense of the intellectual's dislocation. Pessimism, as Saltus has it, excises and explains boredom and nausea. The "universal nausea . . . circulating from one end of Europe to the other, presents these symptoms of melancholy and disillusion which, patent to every observer, are indubitably born of the insufficiencies of modern civilization."[23]

The critic, having the advantage of hindsight, can find much of the later Saltus in these two early works. His most damaging judgment is that the Schopenhauerian escape into self became the Saltusian escape, that Saltusian timidity became capitulation. Even at this stage, Saltus, implicitly agnostic or antitheist, is afraid to wound his readers' traditional theism. He therefore plays down the pessimist's rejection of ultra-mundane felicity. He introduces what is to be his lifelong concern with religion, here expressed negatively. He also presents his reader with an escape clause: "Life is not an affliction to those who are, and who can remain young."[24] His escape into beauty or art may be foreshadowed. He demonstrates his obsession with the illusions of love and happiness and evinces not the irrelevancy of social action but an uneven, naïve political sensibility which later hardens into an acceptance of American imperial dreams.

III *"What Pessimism Is Not"*

In his last work on pessimism, an essay entitled "What Pessimism Is Not," Saltus perfectly suits paradox to style and content. He shows the reader in effect that pessimism is the point of view of the paradoxist. He makes it clear that pessimism is not equal to its clichés, that it does not invite suicide, gloom, or pain. In fact, as the central paradox of the essay tells us, it is not the pessimist but the optimist who "takes everything amiss." For the optimist "has any number of big dolls, and their sawdust disconcerts him terribly." The image is excellent. The earnest optimist is, in his earnestness, discomfited by a great deal. He dislikes failure, which Saltus bravely avers is more salutary than success; and, when failure enters the optimist's world, "he dashes his head in the pillow."[25]

What is at issue in this essay is surely an early effort to subvert the American philosophy of "uplift." The pessimist opens his eyes; the optimist shuts his. The latter expects the perfections of Paradise; the former accepts imperfection. The pessimist denies only "one thing . . . that happiness exists"; he knows that pain "is the inevitable concomitant of life." Therefore why accept a golden age of the past? If any such age exists, it is "not behind us, but beyond."[26] Although by the end of the essay the pessimist has come dangerously close to accepting his opposing partner's whatever-is-is-good, the paradoxist remains by definition ambivalent, agile, cunning.

IV The Lords of the Ghostland

What Saltus masks in the serio-comic irony of paradox is his desire to believe. His denomination of pessimism as the "religion of the future" in his earlier books indicates what we would know anyway—that the rejection of traditional religion will involve the search for a replacement.[27] By the time Saltus wrote his next book about religion the mask had dropped. In *The Lords of the Ghostland* (1907) Saltus examines the major religions of the world through nine gods: Brahma, Ormuzd, Amon-Râ, Bel-Marduk, Jehovah, Zeus, Jupiter, and Christ. These "lords of the ghostland" are the gods of the various unseen heavens man has created, and Saltus bows to them; his role is the explicator's not the proselytizer's. The aura and the mystery of the gods persuade and detain him, as random passages indicate. Of Amon-Râ: "He became triune and remained unique. He was Osiris, he was Isis, he was Horus. At once father, mother, and son, he fecundated, conceived, produced, and was." A typical antithesis: "Man, then, for the first time, loved what he worshipped and worshipped what he loved."[28] So man related to Zeus. Christ, no longer the exponent of pessimism he was in the early works, is still special and daring but not finally too special or too daring.

What sharply distinguishes this book from his earlier works on pessimism is Saltus' concern with doctrines of reincarnation and transmigration. He is already more than tempted by the doctrines of theosophy. While pessimism had to be discussed within the context of society and history, theosophy permits Saltus to discuss the soul in relation to eternity and so to leave the temporal far behind. The ethics of Christianity he had never attacked. Not only in *The Anatomy of Negation* and in *The Philosophy of Disenchantment* but in the essay, "What Pessimism Is Not," he had spoken of "the abnegation of self" which he traced as far back as Buddhism. His version of pessimism stresses the stoic side of Christianity.

Saltus has not changed from a non-believer into a believer; he is always a believer. He had expected pessimism to become the religion of the future; it had not. Moreover, pessimism could not serve a man who needed some divinity in his substitute religion, and that he chose theosophy is not entirely surprising. Yet no one could have been more sceptical of theosophy than Saltus or more ironic about its pretensions. In 1896, he had irreverently reported the doings of a Theosophist Congress in New York: Theosophists, he said,

> have a few things to remember and a great many to forget—to forget among other things that we have any use for esoteric doctrines, and to remember that Buddhism, of which their creed is an offshoot, was one of the simplest of the religions of the world, a plain law for plain men, one in which there was nothing occult, one which as taught by the founder had no legerdemain or mahatmas in it, one which exacted of the adherent little more than sincerity and sobriety and a belief in the final remission of

> sin. If it has become more complex since, the fault lies with such people as the Theosophists, who seem to think that, being ninnies themselves, there must be plenty more just like them.[29]

These "ninnies" were, some ten years later, to acquire their detractor's respect. Actually, however, Saltus makes no great parade of his interest in theosophy and never actively propagandizes for it. He allows it to enter into two of his novels (*The Monster*, 1912; *The Ghost Girl*, 1922) and into *The Lords of the Ghostland;* but its presence is generalized and never central. He never approaches theosophy with the energy and enthusiasm he gave to pessimism. He could not use it to get new ideas or to shape a point of view.

Intense involvement with religion characterizes the rebellious literary elements of the later nineteenth century; and these rebellious elements were precisely those repelled by the nineteenth-century faith in observable fact. Whether that involvement shows itself as virulent anti-Christianity (the earlier Marquis de Sade is a perfect illustration) or as conversion to Catholicism, the involvement is present. France produced more skeptics than England which produced the Oxford Movement. In Joris Karl Huysmans, so central an example of the sensibility of the 1890's, the two faces are joined: the blasphemer and the believer are one. Even by the end of *A Rebours* (1884), Huysmans' interest in religion is apparent and his subsequent conversion to Catholicism not a surprise. Blasphemer and believer are united in their revulsion against pseudo-religion, in their agonizing sense of betrayal by an ideal. The painful discrepancy between the ideal and the fact makes the blasphemer. That discrepancy may also return him to belief.

It would certainly be a species of snobbery to accept theosophy in Yeats and to reject it in Saltus. It is more useful and more accurate to recognize why such systems attracted writers. In the same column in which Saltus lampoons theosophy, he notices with interest Dr. Pierre Janet's work on multiple selves, on hypnosis, on other inner caves and corners of the self. He had also been interested in von Hartmann's concept of the Unconscious. Saltus indicates in certain of his novels and in much of his writing an interest in multiple selves, in buried selves, and in any mystery of human nature and motivation. He sensed, he doubtless knew from his own experience, the existence of inner demons that the idea of progress did not include, that biological evolution had for the moment to bypass, that the major currents of investigation had bypassed—whether he did or did not read Freud's *Interpretation of Dreams* which appeared in 1899.

Theosophy represented a faith in the power of the unseen and the intangible, a faith in the supremacy of the imagination over the machine. The twentieth century may need to extricate itself from the reverse fallacy. It may need to relearn the power of the conscious in relation to the unconscious.[30] But Saltus saw, as any sensitive observer of the nineteenth century could not fail to see, that the data now partially subsumed in the pioneer disciplines of psychology and psychoanalysis were those his century ignored or suppressed.

What Saltus could not generate was a sufficient degree of commitment to either pessimism or theosophy or to a personal set of convictions. He needed a stronger inner demon than he had and a stronger, more intelligent response from his environment. But what he saw and what he needed other contemporaries had also seen and needed. Greater men, like William James and Henry Adams, had spoken from a basically similar sense of the special destructiveness of modern life. The Saltus visions and needs were not isolated.

CHAPTER 3

Studies in Ornamental Disenchantment

Golden lads and girls all must,
As chimney sweepers, come to dust.
Cymbeline

SALTUS' FIRST WORKS were critical studies which placed him as a supporter of fictional realism and philosophical pessimism. He seemed to have embarked upon a career as critic rather than novelist. Yet a few years after his appreciation of Balzac was published, Saltus brought out a novel which owed very little to the French novelist. *Mr. Incoul's Misadventure* was the first of fifteen published novels and more than thirty short stories. Saltus also tried a playlet and poetry. The poems, always short and frequently in sonnet form, were collected from notebooks, periodicals, and newspapers by Marie Saltus and posthumously published.[1] His output was considerable.

I *Novels: 1887-1895*

He was especially prolific in the seven years between 1887 and 1894 when he wrote more than half of his total fictional output. Carl Van Vechten aptly spoke of Edgar's fictions as "experiments in decorative irony" and as "pessimistic allegories."[2] Indeed, for the word "misadventure" in his first novel, *Mr. Incoul's Misadventure* (1887), the reader may justifiably substitute "disenchantment," since disenchantment is almost an obsession in Saltus' fiction. In *Incoul*, Saltus splits his irony and his allegory for the first and only time between two heroes, a husband and a lover. The husband, Harmon Incoul, plots his revenge upon his presumably guilty wife and her partner-in-crime, Lenox Leigh.

In this version of the traditional crime passionel, passion, if it is present, is cold and governed by a highly formal, obsessive morality. Lenox Leigh begins as a shallow, well-bred, penniless young man; before long he has become a disenchanted victim and a spokesman for philosophic pessimism. The lover falls easily before the silent, malignant glitter of the husband, his millions, and his possessiveness. The novel as a whole reveals the strong Saltus preoccupation with infidelities and misunderstandings, particularly with circumstantial errors in the love between men and women.

In the action of the novel, Maida Barhyte is forced to accept the proposal of Incoul, a widowed New York millionaire of middle age, because her mother knows how poor they are and because Lenox Leigh only proposes a liaison without marriage. (Lenox wants Maida actively only when she is safely married.) Maida accepts Incoul on the condition that their marriage will remain unconsummated. (They are aware of a similar compact in Balzac's *Eugénie Grandet.*) Excited by the prospect of having to win a woman already his wife, Incoul accepts on condition that the agreement not be considered absolute. Maida slowly comes to respect Incoul's moral austerity and his financial plenty; when Maida and Lenox meet once again and give Incoul cause for suspicion, the reader never suspects Incoul's satanic plan of punishment.

Later Leigh, his honor ruined by a ruse of Incoul's, commits suicide with a self-injected overdose of laudanum. Maida, faithful to Incoul and dressed for her true bridal night, takes death as her consummation when her bridegroom feeds her an overdose of bromide of potassium. She appears to accept death as deserved; for, having loved before, she is impure and shopworn. His revenge complete, Incoul cool and taciturn, is about to examine his financial accounts as the novel closes.

Whether he appears as "a modern hunter of the Holy Grail," or, more accurately, as a kind of early Roman striated with diabolism, Incoul convinces.[3] Leigh, who degenerates to drinking absinthe (he once drank only claret and water) and to consorting with a French ballet dancer, is interesting but inconsistent and a lightweight foil for Incoul even after his conversion to pessimism. The culmination of Incoul's revenge in crime shares the focus of the novel with the degeneration of young Leigh. Leigh's several patrician selves (the genteel poor playboy, the man of letters, the Southern aristocrat) and Incoul's cool and rigorous power—all cry for a rich, ironic examination of the mores and manners of upper-class New York in the 1880's.

Although Saltus is not a novelist of manners, he does give the reader a sense of upper-class habits. Maida and Incoul have a traditional European honeymoon, and they frequent popular cosmopolitan and resort centers like London, Paris, Baden-Baden, Biarritz, and San Sebastian. Like Vevey in Henry James's *Daisy Miller,* Baden-Baden is polyglot. Russians, English, Brazilians, and Americans come together there to play. It is a life but vaguely rocked by the news of a Wall Street crash. Incoul, like his fellow vacationers, is rich enough to survive crash after crash. Wherever the Incouls go, they rent houses or villas and become a part of indigenous as well as visiting society. In names like Mrs. Bunker Hill and Mrs. Nicholas Manhattan, Saltus suggests in a lighter fashion than in the novel as a whole his attitude toward upper-class New York society.

One of the bravura descriptions in the novel, the description of a corrida in San Sebastian, is accurate, thorough, and engrossing—and probably the first full-length description of a corrida in an American novel. The Incouls and another American family find their appetites whetted by a ladies' bullfight at Saint-Jean-de-Luz. This corrida, where heifers are baited and there is no death, is a prologue to the true corrida at San Sebastian, as is the description of the black Goya drawings and the esoterica in the library of the Biarritz villa the Incouls have rented. The first corrida is fully described, from the arena itself to the traditional opening ritual to the "last act of the first of the wonderful cycle" of the six dramas of the afternoon. After the corrida the author reports: "As a topic, the bull-fight was inexhaustible. Every thread of conversation led back to it."[4] When, at the corrida's end, Maida sees Lenox amid the spectators for the first time since her marriage, the corrida assumes a purpose. It prepares for the future violence in the novel, even if that preparation is surface and tonal.

When Lenox describes his arrival in Irun on a crowded train

and the arrest of an irate Frenchman and remarks, "If the Frenchman had only been shot before their eyes it would indeed have been a charming prelude to a bull-fight," we are reminded of *The Sun Also Rises.*[5] In that novel Hemingway provides "the charming prelude" Leigh wanted: a man is trampled to death during the encierro at Pamplona as a deliberately absurd prelude to the corrida's deliberately ritualized death.

Saltus declines, as suggested earlier, a fuller examination of the degeneration (or exaltation) of Lenox Leigh; he also declines fuller integration of setting and event with motivation. When Lenox underlines his regret that the Frenchman had not been shot with, "I never saw a man shot," the reader wonders and half expects that Saltus will provide him with the experience; but the remark remains only that.[6] Thus, although Saltus has a strong feeling for themes and situations still viable in the contemporary novel (the pain of experience, the wandering American, the involvement with violence), his feeling materializes in a rudimentary way.

If Saltus is more interested in Lenox Leigh's conversion to pessimism and his suicide than in Incoul's diabolism, then Tristrem Varick, the hero of the next novel, is a better example of the victim of innocence, optimism, and youth. More unified than his first novel, *The Truth About Tristrem Varick* (1888) is dedicated to Eduard von Hartmann, "my master, the philosopher of the unconscious," as an "attempt in ornamental disenchantment." Structurally, the novel is more effective and more lucid because the point of view is always the hero's. The plot creaks less; it depends entirely on a single gratuitous assumption.

Tristrem, just returned, Europeanized, from the traditional sojourn abroad after attendance at a prep school in Concord (which can only be Saltus' own St. Paul's) and graduation from college, is startled by a New York that seems shrunken and provincial. His single blindness is his assumption that Viola Raritan, who is "a festival of beauty in the festival of life," either loves him or will come to love him. He assumes that the cause of their broken betrothal is her mistaken belief that they are half-brother and sister. He never imagines she loves his cynical school-chum, Royal Weldon, who has married for money "prettiness and insipidity personified, the sort of a woman that ought to be gagged and kept in bed with a doll."[7] Where Viola is, happiness is; and Viola has left the country. So Tristrem, true to his knightly first name, embarks on a long, dedicated quest for Viola and happiness. Unsuccessful, he learns on his return voyage from a fellow passenger, stuck in to speak for philosophic pessimism, that Viola has had a baby; he divines that Royal is father and villain.

Tristrem's disenchantment is not so complete, however, as it will be. Assuming Viola's emotional imprisonment against her will by Royal, Tristrem still wishes to save her and to marry her. Caught in the exigencies of an archaic code of honor, he cannot stop with her rescue and kills Weldon. A thin exotic stiletto, so thin it leaves no mark and draws no blood, does the job. Although such gimmickry is non-essential in this early Saltus novel, Viola's response to Tristrem's gift is essential: " 'Assassin'," she hisses, " 'I loved him!' "[8] This revelation, which destroys Tristrem's will to live, is, of course, a sardonic comment on his gratuitous gallantry. Although Weldon's death is diagnosed as heart failure, Tristrem gives himself up, refuses to implicate Viola, and will, the reader assumes, be sentenced to death.

The harsh revelation that his beloved Viola still loves her seducer and now despises her savior, which completes Tristrem's disenchantment also highlights two implications about the morality of courtship and love. One is conventional: the villain is an upper-class seducer who married for money and found sexual pleasure outside of marriage. The other is unconventional: an upper-class girl can have an extra-marital affair without social or moral punishment. Furthermore, Tristrem, like Lenox Leigh, somehow escapes the superficiality and corruption of his class, despite his brutal analysis of himself as a leisured dilettante who is incapable of creative, sustained effort and capable only of appreciation.

All three major figures emerge from incomplete families: Tristrem, motherless; Royal, an orphan; Viola, fatherless. Characters with a single or no parents are not unusual in nineteenth-century fiction, as the novels of Dickens and James alone remind us. Such background facts have an inner signification that is bolstered by the suspected incest, the actual *Wanderjahr*, the actual murder, a criminal conviction, and Tristrem's firm, calm desire for death. These details, like Viola's pregnancy, must have upset many Saltus readers. They characterize the Saltus novels, but they are not always so effectively used to exaggerate the discrepancy between the respectable exterior and the crumbling interior of his characters as they are in his two most interesting novels, *Tristrem Varick* and *Incoul.*

Perhaps the most powerfully written portion of the novel is the description of Tristrem's nightmare—in which the ugly face of truth comes prophetically to his unconscious long before the actual confirms and convinces him of the horror of truth. The dream foreshadows events to come. It stands as a tribute to the residue of vision and conviction in Saltus the artist. Somewhere within the surface conception of Tristrem lies the desire to explore the ego-locked personality that insistently imposes its romantic fabric of true love, faith, and honor on the world. What Tristrem calls disillusion is his final, unsupportable recognition that facts other than those he has constructed have an objective existence. The romantic discordance between conception and existence which erupts in violence is the true theme of the Saltus novels.

Saltus also introduces in *Tristrem* his reappearing outside observer, a witty, superficially cynical writer of minor talent who appears in eleven of the novels, seven times as Alphabet Jones, twice as Melancthon Stitt (in *Madam Sapphira,* 1893, and *Enthralled,* 1894) and once as Melancthon Orr (*The Perfume of Eros,* 1905). In his tenth appearance, in the post-humous novel, *Ghost Girl* (1922), the outside-observer-author becomes Chandos Poole, the only first-person narrator in all of Saltus' novels. Rarely does Alphabet Jones perform any serious functional role. The heroes generally meet him at dinner parties or at their club. He is, on occasion, a confidant of some importance. He is frequently ready to *épater le bourgeois.* To the lady who wants to know if literature pays and who is easily persuaded that Bradshaw wrote *Ben Hur* and to the dinner table at large, he says: " 'I would rather have written *Salammbô* than have built the Brooklyn Bridge. It was more difficult, and besides it will last longer'." He often authors epigrams: " 'Your wife would rather be dead than out of fashion'."

Perhaps the following description from *When Dreams Come True* (1895) best illustrates Saltus' deprecating portrait of the author as member of Washington Square society: "The latter was a writer of great promise, which thus far he had failed to fulfill. His name was Jones. As a conversationalist he was inimitable, *blageur* and paradoxical, possessed of that spontaneity which sound so well across a table and which is vapid in black and white."[9] The description is also a portrait of the minor avant-garde writer of the 1890's, and it might be a self-portrait. Certainly unflattering, it describes a fundamentally unserious writer. The romantic self-mockery, transparent and saddening, serves ultimately, as superficial cynicism so frequently does, as a means of evading analysis and development.

Eden Menemon Usselex, the heroine of *Eden* (1888), seems at first to be partly Harmon Incoul and partly Tristrem Varick, destined to self-destruction because she falsely assumes her husband's infidelity. Her happiness depends on her discovery of the truth and on her acceptance of her middle-aged husband's prior marriage and two grown children. Her own past contains a rakish young man. Unexpectedly both husband and wife are allowed a happy ending although they have loved before. The tone of the novel is flatter, but its marital mores are thicker than they are in *Incoul* though not so complicated as in *Tristrem Varick*.

Saltusian heroines tend to fall into two groups: the pure, innocent, puritan Eve to which Eden, by her name and her motto, "Sois sans tache," so clearly belongs, and the experienced, darker, more fascinating Lilith. Only in the later novels does this grouping become antipodal enough to suggest a significant, sometimes slick, use of the light and the dark lady. Claire Bucholz, an interesting new woman, appears in *A Transaction in Hearts* (1889), the first novel which sets up, albeit mutedly, the Eve-Lilith antithesis. Fittingly, she contrasts with her sister Ruth, the wife of Christopher Gonfallon, an Episcopal priest not too long removed from a dull Bronx parish to a fashionable Manhattan one which he owes to the Countess Cinq-Cygne, known as "the heiress of Bronx."

The novel, told entirely from Gonfallon's point of view, is concerned with the priest's inability to conquer the love he feels for his wife's sister. The clergyman as a figure vulnerable to sin represents a conception always daring and always capable of fine, powerful ironies. Gonfallon suffers and sees himself as a Tartuffe, but his sufferings do not abate his passion for his cool, bright sister-in-law who is quite indifferent to his clumsy advances. Claire, involved with her own young man, circumvents Gonfallon at every turn until he must finally officiate at her marriage, after which he gropes "through the darkness to Ruth."[10]

Claire, presented indirectly, has the coolness, the poise, and the wit to handle her brother-in-law's infatuation so that her sister is unaware of its existence. She serves, furthermore, the function of undercutting Gonfallon's pompousness and self-righteousness. When he announces, " 'we prefer that you see only men whose intentions are honorable'," she replies briefly, " 'there aren't any'," laughs, and lets "her head fall back on the cushion."[11] Her stance always has this careless indolence about it, this frankness, this abruptness, this casual posturing that much later becomes characteristic of the flapper or the new woman.

Like Tristrem Varick's, Gonfallon's love for Claire is totally his fabrication. That is why he is caught unaware by the announcement of Claire's impending marriage. Saltus' love-ridden heroes never really see the object of their love and blindly assume their love is returned. Love for these heroes is a kind of self-generated obsession from which it is better, indeed necessary, to be free.

When the Countess Cinq-Cygne, née Chisolm Jones, turns out to have played, in this story of obsessional love, her own mad vengeance against her husband and his lover we are not surprised. Her death reveals a vengeance as Gothic and insane as Miss Havisham's in Dickens' *Great Expectations* or as Miss Emily's in Faulkner's "A Rose for Emily": she has herself beheaded the two offenders and kept their heads hidden in her home for years. The Gothic revenge of the heiress from Bronx is not so outlandish if her minister is himself nearly destroyed with passion.

In his next novel, *The Pace That Kills* (1889), Saltus converts his patrician young hero into a man animated by revenge and greed whose final remorse and suicide seem unreal and merely conventional. Roland Mistrial has the background and looks of Lenox Leigh or Tristrem Varick, the morality of Royal Weldon, and a touch of Mr. Incoul's villainy. Like Lenox Leigh, Roland Mistrial has no fortune and maneuvers to win the hand of Justine Dunellen, a wealthy New York heiress. Since Justine's father refuses his blessing and his millions, the couple elopes.

Mistrial has a nemesis in Guy Thorold, the brother of a former sweetheart who died during an abortion; his wife, Justine, continues faithful to Mistrial even when his behavior is cruel and indifferent. When she bears him a child, he assumes Thorold is the father. Actually, Mistrial had engineered his wife's and Thorold's closeness in order to thwart the will of his now deceased father-in-law which demanded an heir Mistrial assumes he cannot provide. Mistrial's wrong assumption finally turns his wife against him. Her desertion, rather than the failure of his plot to damage Thorold and get the Dunellen millions engenders his self-disgust and suicide. But these familiar elements of the Saltus novel do not here cohere very well. The stark outlines of the monster man and the utterly faithful patient wife fail to light the diabolic glow that suffuses *Mr. Incoul's Misadventure.*

Madam Sapphira (1893), occasioned by Saltus' divorce, substitutes the monster woman for the monster man of *The Pace That Kills.* Hilda Nevius is the schemer and her husband, Carol Nevius, must be disabused of his belief in her integrity. The novel is more interesting because it illuminates Saltus' conception of his first marriage than it is for itself although it turns, as Saltus novels usually do, on the unmasking of an illusion.

The next novel, *Enthralled* (1894), belongs, as we shall see, with Saltus' later novels. *When Dreams Come True* (1895), which follows it, invites more extended discussion for its uniqueness in allowing the young hero ultimately to choose a Lilith for his wife. Tancred Ennever is the perfect Saltus hero: young, well-born, of Dutch-English New York parentage, and a graduate of St. Paul's, Harvard, and Wall Street.[12] The depth of his involvement in the life of letters may make him atypical. Saltus is both mocking and affectionate toward his hero who believes "it is as indecent for a young man to enter the drawing-room of life without a book to his credit as to appear without a cravat."[13] Tancred's simultaneously published first works, sustain even by their titles the light, serio-comic irony (can it be called satire?) of the author's attitude: *Sonnets Serene and Otherwise* and *From Fiji to Venice.* They are to be followed by *The Heroines of Love* which Tancred begins during the action of the novel.[14] The description of the latter work exactly parallels Saltus' own history of love from Helen of Troy to the present in *Historia Amoris,* published eleven years later.

Tancred, more like Saltus than any other of his heroes, has even written papers on Leconte de Lisle and Huysmans during his student years in Paris. His writing originates from his aristocratic ideal of cultivation, for what young man worth his aristocratic salt could not produce a creditable volume of verse or a book of travel impressions? Tancred's name, derived from Voltaire who got it from Ariosto, is as hothouse and protected as his painfully youthful probity. (Tristrem was another knightly named hero.) He predictably, romantically, and totally falls for a young lady, Sylvia Marsh, an Eve type. Sylvia is reticent, undemonstrative—in fact, silent. Because Tancred has no objective demonstration of her reciprocal love, it is no surprise to discover later that she still loves her old flame, Prince Sappia. But Tancred loves her; and, when she finally accepts him, his blind, indulgent self believes she loves him.

Mme. Bravoura, Sylvia's friend, of whom Tancred has heard "that you fascinate and forsake," promises to be a voluptuous serpent lady and ends by being merely mature, witty, intelligent, articulate, vivacious—a welcome contradiction of the expected stereotype. Tancred's information was wrong: she takes some time to fascinate, and he forsakes her. When Sylvia breaks her engagement to Tancred, plunging him into necessary disillusion and an awareness of Sylvia's relative shallowness, Mme. Bravoura, the widow of an American who bought a European title, steps in to fill the gap; but events cause Tancred to mistrust her. After breaking their engagement and undergoing a long apprenticeship in self-examination which includes a hot summer in New York City writing *The Heroines of Love* (no gentleman of his class remains in New York during the summer), he meets her accidentally at Como; they are reunited and blessed by Sylvia and her new husband, Prince Sappia.

What Tancred discovers is that there is no love without reciprocity. In order to recognize reciprocity, Tancred must lose his adolescent preoccupation with self. What the novel presents is a journey from illusion to awareness with every coach stop a painful, partial adjustment of the discrepancy between desire and fact. Tancred must become worthy of Bravoura; when he does, he may marry her. Tancred's suffering, the source of his growth, makes him finally worthy and able to arrive where there is "no place left for self."

The phrase may be exaggerated, but the hero's deliberate choice of a mature, experienced woman was as rare in American fiction then as now. The choice is underlined in the novel because at one point both ladies are free, and he may choose either. Bravoura is a widow, but the real point is that she is experienced sexually. For Saltus to have a virginal, young hero choose such a woman deserves specific emphasis. Bravoura is the only such character in the Saltus canon. The purity obsession of an Incoul, of Maida Incoul herself, and of other Saltus characters is exorcised in *When Dreams Come True* (1895).

II Enthralled *(1894)*

Unfortunately, the later novels develop not from the inner complications of *When Dreams Come True* but from the outer contortions and inner melodrama of *Enthralled* (1894). Although its almost comic extravagance of evil and intrigue seems a parody of Wilde's *The Picture of Dorian Gray* (1891) or of R. L. Stevenson's *Dr. Jekyll and Mr. Hyde* (1886), its plot probably owes more to Hugo's *l'Homme qui rit* (1831-2).

The hero-villain Oswald Quain begins as the monstrously ugly protégé of the millionaire Richard Attersol in love with Myrrha Attersol. When Attersol refuses to accept their marriage, only the reader knows why—this time the possible incest is real, not imagined. Quain's love, at first genuine, soon becomes only a means to the Attersol fortune; Myrrha is merely "aglow with gold," and Quain "not a man but an aim." After a grotesque epiphany, "At once he understood himself. Other men had infirmities, he was sound—no gastritis called good taste, none of that obesity of the mind which is known as decorum, no rheumatism of the nerves, none of the anchylosis of rectitude. He was an ambition animated."[15]

But the obsessiveness described, common enough in American literature, seems tacked on, exterior. With his accomplice Isaacstein, Quain engineers and executes the murder of Attersol, who has cut off his allowance, then flees, fabricates a suicide at sea, has his face and body transformed by a London surgeon, and returns as the Earl of Cloden to woo Myrrha and her millions. Myrrha has more than millions: "Her own people had been notable at a time when Union Square was a suburb," a fact that barely interests Quain.[16] Of course, her aunt cannot contain her delight at the prospect of her niece's marrying royalty. And, of course, the loyal family doctor, the rival suitor for Myrrha's hand, unmasks the villain just in time. Quain dies as Myrrha learns what Quain had never known: he is her half-brother.

Quain is a reversal of Hugo's hero, Gwynplaine, whose natural beauty is apparent everywhere but in his face. That face, deformed in infancy by the "surgical sculpture" of the Comprachicos (the Childbuyers), forever presents an automatic grimace, a mask like the one of ancient comedy. Gwynplaine is also a symbol of socially mutilated mankind as Quain never is. The description of Quain's development leaves unclear whether or not he represents natural evil or environmentally developed evil. His natural ugliness may or may not represent, therefore, an acceptance of a congruence between the physical and the moral. Where Gwynplaine is born fair and made ugly by man, Oswald Quain is born ugly and made fair by man. Gwynplaine's deformity was not self-motivated; he is victimized. Quain's alteration is self-engineered and meant to deceive.

The character of Quain, the Saltus medium for a study of evil, reflects, like Dorian, a conflict about, even a fear of, the total consciousness the hero and the author profess to crave. Like Dorian, like des Esseintes, Quain is seduced by literature. When he finishes his apprenticeship to philosophy, he is thoroughly amoral: "even the prejudice of a prejudice had gone. He was unable to take anything seriously, least of all himself. He was *fin de siècle*, last train, and hurrah for the hindmost."[17] Intellectual liberation ends, ironically, in monomania and murder.

Quain does not undergo the severe struggle Stevenson exteriorizes by giving Hyde a separate existence. Nevertheless, beyond the claptrap machinery of Oswald's plastic surgery lies a similar need to exteriorize dichotomy. For Attersol can father a beast and a beauty, a Hyde and a Jekyll who do not even know they are related. The reader knows and that is enough. An awareness of the primitive, the amoral or the id element in man, is not limited to the Naturalistic novel. Beauty is fascinated by the beast, loving him out of dread rather than happiness. The closeness of good and evil is underscored when these would-be lovers are made brother and sister and thus forever linked, even though Myrrha has not cooperated in Quain's crime.

The novel may well represent Saltus as mocker and exorciser of his own commitment to *fin de siècle* modes. It is unusually bad unless it is accepted as comic exaggeration. Saltus may well have laughed as he concocted and launched this conglomeration of pseudo-characters and pseudo-events. He certainly spends a great deal of ludicrously loving time on the precise, literal details of Quain's metamorphosis—how his ears were altered, his arms shortened, his legs lengthened—in a parody of sensational journalism and advertising promises. It remains, nonetheless, difficult to know whether the novel has a comic purpose.

III *The Later Novels (1895-1922)*

For ten years, between 1895 and 1905, Saltus wrote no novels. Most of the six novels he wrote between 1905 and his death have convoluted plots and stick figures. One character describes the events of *Ghost Girl* (1922) as "illustrations for an unwritten tale of Hoffman, etchings for some story lost or strayed from the portfolio of Villiers de l'Isle Adam, vignettes for an unpublished manuscript of Poe." Neither these honorific allusions to the writers whose effects Saltus would like to achieve nor the the twins, the living-dead girl, the psychic lady, one hero's spider-shaped birthmark, the seances, the empty coffins—none of these classic elements of Gothic horror makes us feel the mystery and terror of life. Death releases Jim Bradish from life, "from those halls hung with enigmas, tapestried with tears, before which the sphinx in flight gallops like a jackal."[18] Although the enigma of existence is what Saltus would like to convey by his convolutions of events, he does not succeed.

In *The Perfume of Eros* (1905) Saltus is less gymnastic. The novel is memorable chiefly for its use of two new women, the incipient flapper and the lower-class girl whose eventual professional success begins with her fall from virtue. The complicated plot involving two upper-class couples and a lower-class mistress has little to recommend it. Only Marie Durand, the lower-class mistress led on by her seducer with promises of marriage, develops as a character. By the time she realizes Royal Loftus will never marry her, she has transcended her apprenticeship to upper-class manners and preoccupations (she has, like some minor Galatea, learned how to eat, how to dress, what to say), and become articulate enough to confront Loftus directly and thoroughly, fling his pay-off of twelve thousand dollars out the window, and take off for Europe quite on her own to continue her voice training.

The Saltus reader remembers Viola Raritan of *Tristrem Varick,* also a singer and also a partner in an unorthodox love affair, but her seducer's social equal. Her social class is unorthodox; her profession is not, for acting and singing have a long association with "libertinism." They are also a traditional means of social advancement. When we see Marie just once more at the end of novel, the ignorant slum daughter of a Gay Street tailor is singing Amneris in *Aida.* She has become a first-class opera singer.

But the wages of sin for Fanny Price, the flapper of the novel, is death. Fanny, always in love with the handsome hero-villain, Royal Loftus, finally gives up waiting for his proposal and marries Annandale. Like Lenox who loved Maida Barhyte, Royal loves Fanny; unlike him, Royal has plenty of money. However, neither man wants the restrictions of marriage. When Fanny, like Maida, or like the typical girl of her class, will not consent to an extra-marital affair, Royal turns to Marie, just as Lenox had turned to the dancer, Mirette. Later, Royal somewhat reluctantly agrees to marry Fanny after her divorce. Royal's murder forestalls that event. Interesting Fanny, witty Fanny, the Pocket Venus (Saltus was known as the Pocket Apollo), has become too difficult to handle. Rather than confront this character in her crisis, Saltus allows her to sicken and die offstage. Thus, within the same novel Saltus is both conventional and bold, both cliché-ridden and perceptive about class mores.

The next novel, *Vanity Square* (1906), promises to present an arresting critique of the ennui inevitable in a sensitive member of the spoiled upper-class of New York. The hero, Gerald Uxhill, who has "written a sequence of sonnets that is quoted still," wearies with the ease and the vanity of his life and of his class. At this point, Saltus injects his own comment, rare for him, of Uxhill's rebellious spiritual state:

> Uxhill, who was a poet and consequently unfitted to balance

> himself on the tight-ropes of philosophy, rebelled . . . at the life to which circumstances had condemned him. . . . The metropolitan existence of a man of means and no occupation is the most maddening that civilization has devised,—a form of earthly damnation in which you are forced to consort with people who have scandals and stocks for sole topics, and, what is worse, for sole joys . . . He was tired of the whole lot. But what irked him most was his durance in the precinct in which he lived, and which, with Central Park on one side, Madison Avenue on the other, Seventy-second Street for frontier, and the Plaza for approach, is colloquially known as Vanity Square.[19]

This statement, one of the most explicit condemnations by Saltus of his own class and, by indirection, of his place in it, or of the place of any male member of it whose center of propulsion is not scandal and stocks, occurs very early in the novel. The reader not unfairly assumes a most interesting struggle or solution will occur within the man of means to find an occupation. For the New York City folklorist, the ascription of the name "Vanity Square" to the still luxurious upper East Side is of interest. It tells us that by 1906 the man of means could range far from Washington Square. The name also underscores Uxhill's boredom and the reader's expectation of an incisive exploration of it. Furthermore, Saltus effectively titles Part I: "The Man Who Did Not Exist."

Soon after the opening line, "When the last guest had gone, Uxhill, with a yawn of boredom unrelieved, dropped into a chair," Saltus describes the hero's wife in the excessively mannered mode of his later work: "She had the face of a fay, the waist of a willis, hair of burnt orange, and vesuvian eyes." Despite these exotic charms, Maud Uxhill, simple and content with her husband and daughter, "innately epictetan [sic], was satisfied with things as they were."[20] To the surprise of the reader, Gerald is ultimately shaken out of his boredom into a new appreciation of all that he is and has. He especially learns to appreciate Maud by contrast with the vampire Lady Stella Sixmith, who is using the exotic poison, orsere (the maid confuses it with horsehair) to eliminate Maud and her daughter so she may marry a millionaire. Although Stella's plans miscarry, she escapes unpunished to become Lady Finsbury.

The discussion of ideas, like the discussion of aberrant mental illnesses, comes to nothing in the novel. Reincarnation, evolution, mythology—the ideas are never integrated. Stella, who joins Hilda Nevius of *Madam Sapphira* as one of Saltus' very few female villains, begins as a very bright conversationalist, even as a philosophical pessimist: " 'God surely is unaware of our existence. Otherwise there would be no pain, no poverty. He would not let sorrow and suffering be'." We may ask if her ideas condemn her, or if her villainy, like Oswald's, is connected with daring intellectual speculation. Unfortunately, the answers are barely suggested in the novel which, like the fairy-tale, ends with and-to-this-day-no-one-knows "the true story of the miracle of Vanity Square."[21] Thus what promised to be a dissection of the useless lives of the denizens of Vanity Square ends as an exemplum of a happy marriage that has survived the machinations of evil. The title is finally inappropriate.

In *Daughters of the Rich* (1909), the setting is for the first time partially in southern California. The inner content of its events is typical Saltus: a man is disillusioned, traumatized as a result, and in this case survives rather than dies with insight. There is again murder and misunderstanding, and two new women (one with orange hair) who can only be considered caricatures by comparison with Saltus' earlier Fanny and Claire. One of the women in *Daughters of the Rich* is murdered and the other is pleased to marry the murderer, her first and never-forgotten lover. An unconsummated marriage recalls Saltus' very first novel, *Incoul*, and Sally Kandy's training "in the international steeplechase of marriage" recalls other heroines and other marriages.[22] Although *Daughters of the Rich* is one of two Saltus novels which were turned into films, it cannot charm the fan of the earlier Saltus novels.

In *The Monster* (1912) Saltus combines suspected incest with two unconsummated marriages. Incest, suspected but non-existent and the monster of the title, prevents the consummation of the marriage of Gulian and Leilah who are honeymooning at Coronado Beach. Leilah runs away—not the first Saltus heroine to leave her man—and Gulian chases her to Europe where she has become Mme. Barouffska. After conversations about theosophy (its first appearance in a Saltus novel), general shenanigans, and two duels, the hero and heroine are reunited. Barouffski dies in the second duel, conveniently, by a hand other than

Gerard's. We learn that Leilah has kept herself pure: " 'I have no more been his wife than I was yours'."[23] Theosophy has sustained her since the disturbing though mistaken revelation that she and Gulian are siblings. The ideal of purity that the obsessive Mr. Incoul maintained becomes in this novel mere ballast, mere magazine-level purity. It is hard to connect with the mores of international society in Paris and Deauville.

Only the Wildean wit of a minor character, Aurelia, whose foil is the slow-witted English lord she calls "Buttercups," suggests the more fecund earlier Saltus. After Aurelia gives up Buttercups and proposes to Prince Farnese who of course accepts, she is still herself: " 'Do you know, I have always thought that constancy must be due either to a lack of imagination or else of opportunity'."[24] Such oases cannot be said to refresh *The Paliser Case* (1919) which is a poor reworking of *The Perfume of Eros* (1905).

IV *Short Stories*

The short stories are characteristically more extreme than the novels in their emphasis on bizarre characters and plots. They are also more frequently comic, even outlandish. Many have an intensity or unity of effect often missing in the novels because they are written in the first person, and the I-narrator is almost always a writer who is patient, curious, and capable of listening. He is usually nameless, usually at work on a book, perhaps on ancient Peru; on a history of the empresses of Rome; or on a more general history of the princesses of the past. Once he reads Epictetus and uses his reading to comment on the action of the story.

Saltus seems not to have realized the value of technical experimentation in his fiction, for he shows no desire to make new forms. He shows his need to satirize or to stretch existing technique only in his extravagant manipulation of plot details. He has no real interest in character or in character development. The writer's inevitable concern with the discrepancy between appearance and reality particularizes itself in these stories, as in the novels, in fakes, fabrications, and lies. The plots show an interest in abnormal psychology, in pathology, in twilight states; the delusions of the novels have become more pathological, more bizarre. In one story a man fabricates a bride, her death, and his subsequent life with her resurrected ghost-like self who appears daily to him; she is his alma Adorata. In another story a magnificent woman turns out to be a mechanical robot, a doll created and kept by a rich Peruvian. Poisons like muscarine and rafflesia appear. Saltus finds rafflesia "hideous yet fascinating, as monstrosity ever is,"[25] yet in only one story and in one novel (*Enthralled*) does Saltus objectify the Hyde self for examination. He isn't really interested in exteriorizing monstrosity. His monsters are normally inner ones.

For his interest in pathology does not displace the concerns of his novels. Infidelity in love occurs frequently in these stories obviously written for publication in popular magazines. Behind the gimmicks and the ground-out prose lies the material for major works: pathology, deception, *crimes passionels,* revenge. The social background is also pertinent since international marriages are more frequent than in the novels. The settings, reminiscent of later international novels, are more foreign than native: Paris, Biarritz, Cuba, Sumatra. Trella Verelst and Shane Wyvil (those incredible names again) in "The Dear Departed" meet in Monte Carlo where "kings, outlaws, demi-reps, professional beauties, cheap trippers and Spanish grandees" congregate. That air, that "smell of vitriol and violets, of vice, patented, prodigal, and perfumed" is a perfect setting for the "sesame of her dollars," of anyone's dollars.[26] Boston and Fifth Avenue have not disappeared nor has the provincial; the Sultan of the Sierras who made his money in muskrats and lake steamers appears but is, incomprehensibly, from Michigan. The great figures of Manhattan society are Bleecker Bleecker, "the richest man out of mythology," or Nicholas Manhattan, or Mrs. Bunker Hill. The type casting is obvious but frequently delightful.

The Saltus fascination with the glitter that could have become his true subject matter seems at first glance to sit a little uneasily with his fascination for crime and pathology. Murder trials, real or suspected poisonings, robot ladies—these extremes are not too strange an extension from the infidelities which seem to be his real obsession. He also shows a gift for comic extravagance in his stories. One heroine (reminiscent of Oscar Wilde's Lady Agnes) in "The Top of the Heap," cannot speak; she can only miaow under excitement. "The Terrible Wedding," filled with the clutter and clatter of a zany Marx Brothers movie, ends as the newlyweds leap out of a burning house, the bride hobbling along, unable to run because her skirt is too tight. One work, really a short story, *The Facts in the Curious Case of Hugh Hyrtl, Esq.* (1892), creates a fragile fable quality that recalls Max Beerbohm's *The Happy Hypocrite* (1896). Poor artist and poor sweetheart eventually become rich; they are already good and beautiful.

Perhaps the best example of first-person narration in the Saltus canon is the new woman's narration of her search for the right man in "A Maid of Modern Athens." Her talk, a comic monologue to an unknown listener, is about her hunt for love and the proddings of Fanny Bunker Hill that she marry. When one suitor quotes the "two souls with but a single thought" line, she suggests "that that must mean half a thought apiece." From her final suitor, a big game hunter who gives her no poetry, no Fichte, and no Spencer, she learns the meaning of love. During a leopard hunt, Ferris Stitt senses that his lady does not want the two magnificent leopards who are "caressing each other with amber insatiate eyes" to be killed, and they are not. This moment of wordless communication causes the maid's surrender. The terse, witty sensibility of this Saltus American heiress makes the end of her search amusing and convincing. Our "Joan of Arc in a tailor-made gown" who found her mate without a mother's assistance and who cared not at all for the opinions of other people shows her beauty, wit, and independence to advantage.[27]

V *Reprise*

In his fiction Saltus toys uneasily with the differences and/or similarities between the fabrications of daily life and those of the artist. In life, they profoundly disturb his essentially romantic interior. In art, they delight him enough so that he can make fictions, but not enough to allow him to dominate or distance his disappointments. His fiction seems less allied to that of the decadents than to the formulas of the detective story, because he is too fixedly fascinated by the circumstantial, as Gorham Munson perceived: "In his short stories and novels Saltus uses mechanized plots and mechanized characters with ingenious variations. Stripped of all but a synoptic verbiage, his stories, appeal to the same naïveté in us which makes 'mystery' or detective stories so popular."[28] Saltus had a gift for popular entertainment. In another era he could have indulged that gift freely without creating disturbances about his value and his place.

It has been easy to say that the New York which Saltus portrays is one with the vices and manners of decadent Rome. His *Imperial Purple* tempts that judgment. In fact, the morality of the novels is essentially traditional. Neither Saltus nor Oscar Wilde quite demonstrated in fiction the courage of his amorality. Nevertheless, Saltus' interest in crime, pathology, and love (today the word would be "sex"), major themes, ancient themes, can stir us still. Of more specific interest to the American novel is his central insistence that experience divest the hero of illusion. The love his characters embrace is almost always a self-generated obsession. Disenchantment becomes, therefore, crucial to growth. Unfortunately, few of his heroes can survive disenchantment. This subject, which gleams strongly through every mechanized device he indulged in, unites Saltus with novelists in the mainstream of American literature.

His New York girls, in their obedient and gleaming, as well as in their independent, "new" selves, are sometimes more engaging than his deluded men. Except for Incoul, his satanic figures are less detaining. In his women, in his men, even in his self-deprecative writers, whether they are called Jones, Stitt, Orr, or Poole, he often shows and enjoys the glittering surface of Vanity Square life. At his best, he also suggests the divided and deluded subsurface of that life.

The adjective "ornamental" is like the Saltus disclaimer that he had not undertaken to prove anything. It suggests that the reader need not take him serously; but this disclaimer could be used radically and fruitfully. The ornamental is neither necessarily "art for art" (there is no such art) nor superficial. It could have served Saltus in his need to analyze illusion. When Saltus came to rely on clotted melodrama, he betrayed his need to investigate the irrational underside of human behavior. Perhaps his self-measurement bears some of the blame, for it was, unfortunately, uneasy, fluctuating and faulty. Saltus could not quite give himself up to the comic or to the extravagant, which he might have been able to master. He sensed the great themes of our time, but he could not do them justice in art. He was, as

Henry James might say, insufficiently saturated with his idea.

Several novels deserve readers, among them: *Incoul, Tristrem Varick, A Transaction in Hearts,* and *When Dreams Come True;* for in these works Saltus makes effective fables. His deluded young patrician men, his lovely girls, and his strangely satanic Incoul combine to give us a sense of the disaster they all court—one built into a way of life that does not prepare for life, that makes delusion and division inevitable.

CHAPTER *4*

Style: The Problem and the Practice

There was a time when America almost had its decadent age.

B. K. H., Providence, R.I., *Journal*,
April 21, 1920.

IN ENGLAND it was "*fang de-seeaycle*" that did it, "my dear, and education, and reading French." In the United States it was "*fin de seekle*," but it undid rather than did it.[1] The few writers who tried to do it in America, Edgar Saltus, Vance Thompson, Walter Blackburn Harte, Percival Pollard, even James Huneker, and several little magazines, like the *Chap-Book*, *M'lle New York*, the *Lark*, didn't do it very well or for very long. The movement here was so slight that its works lack even the minor eminence achieved by those of the English 1890's. American writers of the 1880's and 1890's lacked a reasonably sympathetic climate of opinion and a public sizeable enough to encourage as well as resist. Their public was all resistance, an ignorant resistance that could only blight. Gelett Burgess, who authored the purple-cow limerick, called it "a decade of small things"; Mencken, a "pianissimo revolt."

I *The Problem*

"Doing it" meant having style. All of Saltus' critics unite in agreeing that Saltus had it. "Style," as Gorham Munson put it, "is a synonym for Saltus."[2] Although the word carried a peculiar magic in the period, it was never subjected to precise definition. Used easily and frequently, "style" as well as "stylist" must have carried an assumed content for both reader and critic no longer current today. We do not say of a writer, "He is a stylist." We do use style but not in inevitable conjunction with stylist. In the 1890's "stylist" often meant little more than the precious or the epigrammatic writer. When Frank Norris said, "Who cares for fine style!" he was reflecting that part of the period which had grossly bifurcated matter and manner in assuming that style was manner without matter.

The terms had other implied or explicit antipodal synonyms: robust-effete; Realist/Naturalist-dandy/esthete; marketplace-ivory tower. The bifurcation was not always obvious or even inevitable. It was probably not even the same in England and in the United States, or even within the United States. Nor was it the same in popular and in "serious" criticism.

The Saltus statement on style, quoted so frequently, perhaps too frequently, first appeared in 1891. It was expanded in 1898 for a *Collier's Weekly* column:

> There are a thousand ways of expressing a given idea, there is but one which is exact. The artist always finds it. He never tangles a sentence with a metaphor. Yet if a foreign term is more precise than a long-winded equivalent he is not an artist if he does not use it. In connection with this it may be noted that in literature only three things count: style, style polished, style repolished. Style may be defined as the harmony of syllables, the fall of sentences, the infrequency of adjectives, the absence of metaphor, the pursuit of a repetition even unto the thirtieth and fortieth line, the use of the exact term no matter what that term may be. These imagination and the art of transition aid but do not enhance. Grammar is an adjunct. It is not an obligation. No grammarian ever wrote a thing that was fit to read.[3]

Usually excerpted for quotation is the remark that only "style, style polished, style repolished" matters. Even so generalized a remark on the necessity for craftsmanship was rare in 1890. And, although Saltus does not make the connection, there is one in England between the emphasis on style and the concurrent interest in applied arts like bookbinding, cabinetmaking, architecture and book illustration, as Holbrook Jackson so well documents in his effort to topple the ivory tower notion of English Decadence.[4]

While America, as she was to do until the twentieth century, followed England later and at a remove in quality and quantity, she too produced men in the fine and applied arts who demonstrated a passion for what Thorstein Veblen was to call "the instinct of workmanship." That instinct needed to be nourished as much in those who worked with words as in those who worked in stone, wood, or steel. Unfortunately, even younger Realists and Naturalists were to elect the debilitating swagger that powerful matter needed only to show itself to be valuable. It could ignore or discard craftsmanship. Somehow craftsmanship had acquired an effete connotation in literature that it never had in art or music.

Saltus, bred on Balzac, Flaubert, the brothers Goncourt, Leconte de Lisle, Baudelaire, and Hugo could hardly reject craftsmanship. Their example suffuses his strictures on style as they were to suffuse twentieth-century literary platforms. His stress on the precise, the exact word is recognizably Flaubert. To assert that prose be bare of metaphor or niggardly of adjective is to suggest a style that Twain and Hemingway could approve of. "The harmony of syllables, the fall of sentences" are, however, more elusive qualities. The allowance of foreign terms is defensible, if it consorts with the first and the basic requirement of precision.[5]

What seems most unusual is "the pursuit of a repetition even unto the thirtieth and fortieth line." Saltus' practice testifies that his conception of repetition is not Gertrude Stein's or Ernest Hemingway's, for it may mean, as we shall see, the use of parallel structure. What is so curious is how close, on the face of it, Saltus comes in this paragraph to the principles Stein and Hemingway were to embody. He even insists elsewhere, as Ezra Pound did, that "good prose is more difficult, and by the same token more rare, than good verse."[6]

What is there to connect the Saltus of this statement with the one famous for epigrams and an eccentric vocabulary? No reader could expect from such a theoretician the style that Percival Pollard was later to call "verbal vertigo." Indeed, the reader who more accurately expects a clean, bare style will find it in early Saltus. Apparently, therefore, the Joris Karl Huysmans style, "le style tachété et faisandé"—"high-flavored and spotted with corruption," as Arthur Symons, the definer of the "The Decadent Movement in Literature" translates the phrase—is not the Saltus style.[7] His is more Flaubertian and Parnassian.

Nowhere does Saltus discuss the epigram. When he undertakes to define wit and to separate it from humor, his definition, given his grounding in French literature, is predictable. For wit is, self-confessedly, one of the characteristics that makes the superiority of French literature: "Humor is merely the commonplace in fancy dress. . . . Wit, on the other hand, presupposes a quantity and quality of intellect which approaches very nearly to genius."[8] Wit, connected as it should be with intellect, but not primarily associated with epigram, becomes the emetic American literature needs.

Wilde and Beardsley come closer to the Huysmans practice than Saltus. Wilde delighted in "unfamiliar imagery and incongruous colour words," in the display of purple patch, preciosity, epigram, paradox and conceit."[9] Undoubtedly, a part of the *faisandé* ideal for its practitioners in England and France is the *frisson* or shudder; and Saltus used these words frequently. It was surely a part of the special vocabulary of the *avant-garde;* Wilde writes to Saltus: "You have given me that *nouveau frisson* I am always looking for."[10] The "shivers," "aigrettes," and "acuity" that Saltus talked of sound very much like *nouveaux frissons.*

In a personal notebook Saltus adopts, predictably, the conviction that style is a jealous divinity: "To do good work, work that will endure, style must be a divinity, a very jealous one too, one that permits no other worship, one that forces you to shut in every passion, inclination and desire in cages where for distraction you may perhaps now and then be suffered to go and see how they are." Such artistic asceticism parallels his insistence on precision which he describes in the same notebook in predominantly angular imagery: style must contain "the rhythm of verse and the precision of mathematics. It should have in it the shivers of harps, aigrettes of flame and convey an idea with the acuity of a knife."[11] The exotic intensity of the similes suggests that Saltusian precision can come to mean a polish and a tonal register so high as to be unbearable. A register so high may paradoxically relate precision to preciosity.

The jealous divinity sometimes relaxes, for at other times Saltus suggests that geniuses often write badly and are exempt from slavery to form as second-order writers are not.[12] The point of view is encountered frequently enough in Romantic theory; it may back up uncomfortably against the polish-polish-polish-again concept of style. Saltus comfortably sustained, however, the paradox of "freedom" for the genius and "slavery" in the form of discipline for the rest—and clearly places himself with the rest.

II *The Practice*

We are perhaps now in a position to examine some specific passages from Saltus' work. What follows is a brief report on the death of a matador which appeared in the popular *Cosmopolitan* magazine:

> Madrid is in mourning. The Plaza de Toros is deserted. The palcos are draped. The toril is empty. Guerrita has gone. He has experienced what I think I have seen described as a change of heart. He has retired from the ring. He was king of it. Rivaled but not excelled by Frascuelo, preceded but not eclipsed by Mazzantini, Guerrita represented the best traditions of toromaquia. It was splendid to see him. He had the grace of Talma, the nerve of Blondin, the agility of Jeffries, the air of a Bourbon and the ease of a ballerina. He played with the bull as a child will play with a kitten. It was not a terror to him, it was a toy. The costume he wore was gorgeous. It was diaphanous too. A pin would have punctured it. In it, with a stick of steel he would invite the attack of a maddened and gigantic brute. A second and the bull would be upon him. Yet in that second the stick of steel would flash, straight over the lowered horns it would sweep, sting down through the parting flesh, touch the seat of life and drop the brute dead in his tracks. That coup, in which he excelled, is regarded as the supreme expression of maestria.[13]

Another briefer, anecdotal paragraph follows. The two paragraphs were never reprinted; they are part of the potpourri end section of the magazine called "Men, Women and Events." As such, they were not written for posterity or for criticism. Because the brief passage is, in a sense, unguardedly written, it has a special value.

Saltus treats his exotic subject relatively simply. He uses an unusually high proportion of short sentences (eleven out of the twenty are six words or less.)[14] The simplicity is only superficial. The longest, the most complicated sentence comes next to last, at the instant of the kill. Its repetition of "stick of steel" occasions a shower of *s* sounds. (The alliteration of *t* and *p* in the preceding sentences is surely deliberate.) By length, structure, and alliteration, this sentence clearly climaxes the matter of the paragraph. Its parallel verbal structure—"sweep," "sting," "touch," "drop"—suggests that, by repetition, Saltus meant parallel structure. He uses parallelism in his two other long sentences: "rivaled but not excelled . . . , preceded but not eclipsed" (verbal elements again) and "the grace of . . . , the nerve of . . . , the agility of . . . , the air of . . . , and the ease of . . ." (nouns here). The opening series of short sentences are also structurally parallel and heavily dependent on the verb "to be."

The diction is not eccentric; in fact, when it falters it does so because it is commonplace as when, in the "maddened and gigantic brute," the choice of "brute" spoils the tone. The foreign "Plaza de Toros," "palcos," and "toril" suit their context; they are not overdone to display the author's knowledge of Spanish or to rely on spurious local color for effect. In violation of his statement on style is the simile (a weak one), "as a child will play with a kitten," and the metaphoric force of the allusions to Blondin, Jeffries, a Bourbon, and a ballerina. Saltus might defend these allusions as necessary before a public ignorant of the art of the bullfight. The "pin" and the "stick of steel" are too antithetic to go well together. The final sentence represents a drop in tone.

The paragraph needs some reworking, but it is essentially a good example of the austere style its maker extolled. A number of the adjectives and the figurative language are weak, but the whole is not. The passage may suggest the need for Saltus to beware of overdoing parallel structure: of piling parallel phrase after parallel phrase or clause. If we compare, however, the simplicity, journalistic perhaps, of this paragraph with a typically convoluted paragraph in Emerson or Melville or Whitman or James, we may agree that, despite the elegances of parallelism, or alliteration, and of diction like "diaphanous," Twain's prose is the paragraph's closest analogue.

In *Mr. Incoul's Misadventure* (1887) the sensuous, exotic passages make a small proportion of the total book. They occur in the description of a library of exotica, its "black" Goyas and black books; of the corrida; in one or two paragraphs of natural descriptions, a sunset or the beach between Biarritz and Saint-

Jean-de-Luz; and in Lenox Leigh's long monologue of despair, a highly literary and abstract one in which he mentions, between sips of absinthe, Menander, Plato, Buddha, Christ, and others. The description of the Goyas and the books (*Les Fleurs du mal* is among them), like the description of the corrida, is non-functional.

These few sensuous sections are pale reflections of Huysmans' catalogues of jewelry, poisons, paintings, or colors. One of the most elaborate sets the scene for the reunion of Maida and Lenox Leigh:

> There is at Biarritz a division of the shore which, starting from the ruins of a corsair's castle, extends on to Saint-Jean-de-Luz. It is known as the Côte des Basques. On one side are the cliffs, on the other the sea, and between the two is a broad avenue which almost disappears when the tide is high. The sand is fine as face powder, *nuance* Rachel, packed hard. From the cliffs the view is delicious: in the distance are the mountains curving and melting in the haze; below, the ocean, spangled at the edges, is of a milky blue. Seen from the shore, the sea has the color of absinthe, an opalescent green, entangled and fringed with films of white, here the mountains escape in the perspective, and as the sun sinks the cliffs glitter. At times the sky is decked with little clouds that dwindle and fade into spirals of pink; at others great masses rise sheer against the horizon, as might the bastions of Titan homes; and again are gigantic cathedrals, their spires lost in azure, their turrets swooning in excesses of vermilion grace. The only sound is from the waves, but few come to listen. The Côte des Basques is not fashionable with the summer colony; it is merely beautiful and solitary. (115)

Sea "the color of absinthe" most obviously localizes the prose in time; the absinthe and the "*nuance* Rachel" sand are the precious elements which prepare us for the elaborate climax of "turrets swooning in excesses of vermilion grace." The passage is a set piece, as are most of Saltus' descriptions; as such, it may be called, as Holbrook Jackson calls *Dorian Gray*, "a piece of literary jewelry," although its glitter is far more subdued and far less characteristic of its total context than Wilde's set pieces.

Gorham Munson asks us not to "be frightened away from Saltus by President Harding's startling predilection for 'The Imperial Purple'."[15] Others shared this predilection and made

Imperial Purple (1892) the best known Saltus work. Its style is less bare but still under control. The book belongs to a genre almost non-existent today—history decked in the colorful impressionism of the magazine essay of the last century. It is history seen as the art of personality, eminently suited to induce delicious shudders. The description of Caesar's triumphal return from Gaul is typical:

> On that day the Via Sacra was curtained with silk. To the blare of twisted bugles there descended to it from the turning at the hill a troop of musicians garmented in leather tunics, bonneted with lions' heads. Behind them a hundred bulls, too fat to be troublesome, and decked for death, bellowed musingly at the sacrifants, who, naked to the waist, a long-handled hammer on the shoulder, maintained them with colored cords. To the rumble of wide wheels and the thunder of spectators the prodigious booty passed, and with it triumphs of war, vistas of conquered countries, pictures of battles, lists of the vanquished, symbols of cities that no longer were; a stretch of ivory on which shone three words, each beginning with a V; images of gods disturbed, the Rhine, the Rhone, the captive Ocean in massive gold; the glitter of three thousand crowns offered to the dictator by the army and allies of Rome. Then came the standards of the republic, a swarm of eagles, the size of pigeons, in polished silver upheld by lances which ensigns bore, preceding the six hundred senators who marched in a body, their togas bordered with red, while to the din of incessant insults, interminable files of prisoners passed, their wrists chained to iron collars, which held their heads very straight, and to the rear a litter, in which crouched the Vercingetorix of Gaul, a great moody giant, his menacing eyes nearly hidden in the tangles of his tawny hair. (20-21)

Although a description of a procession must by definition involve catalogues of objects and persons, the catalogue is, nonetheless, characteristic Saltus. He frequently finds occasion for lists and invests them, as he does here, with a kind of cold sensuousness. The glitter is the cold, metallic one of gold and silver, broken only by the red borders of the senators' togas. Other tactile elements, leather, silk, ivory, add to the sense of the superlative which Saltus presents directly in diction like "too fat," prodigious," "Three thousand crowns," "massive," "swarm," "interminable," and less directly in the details of the procession from the opening band of musicians to the closing files of prisoners with the solitary, the defeated Vercingetorix.

The paragraph carefully works toward its climax, the contrast between defeat and triumph. The final tactile elements, iron and human hair, are one example of that contrast: the iron, a contrast in value and color to the gold and silver of victory; the human hair, despite its tangles, introduces a softness different from the curtain of silk over the Via Sacra. The sound is also carefully constructed, from the opening bugles, the bellowing of bulls, the rumble of wheels to the "thunder of spectators" which is only near the end of the paragraph particularized as "the din of incessant insults" addressed to the prisoners of war. Alliteration occurs frequently: "the blare of . . . bugles," "decked for death," "colored cords," "wide wheels," and "tangles . . . tawny." The "b's" in the opening two sentences are particularly strong.

The sentences are long, but uncomplicated in structure. The construction is loose; phrases, frequently parallel, are added to a single verbal element. The sentence which begins, "To the rumble . . ." is, for example, entirely hung on the verb "passed." The fifth and last sentence, the longest and most complexly constructed, contains the most interesting detail in the entire paragraph, not the iron collars but the fact that these collars made the prisoners hold "their heads very straight." The detail is more than "got up" from historical sources: it is more telling than the more conventional "menacing eyes" and "tawny hair." Above all, it suggests rather than states the pride of the defeated.

The material, exotic enough, does not need and Saltus does not give it an unusual or eccentric vocabulary. The passage is more mannered than the passages on Guerrita and Biarritz, but it is not overripe. It has a certain splendor and richness. It is not yet an example of "Swinburne's fault committed in prose."[16]

That fault, that "style-suicide" or "verbal vertigo," may be more characteristic not only of Saltus' later writings but of his essays and articles than of his novels and his history. The essays and articles appeared in magazines and newspapers, and Saltus may have considered the pyrotechnical approach the wise one for journalistic media. Particularly in his *Smart Set* and *Cosmopolitan* essays does he lavish the reader with epigram and paradox beneath which the bitterness of his own defeat is frequently apparent: "Here, at once, in the land of the brave and the home of the freebooter, coin is obviously suggestive"; "An inability to write anything but cheques is the smart thing here."[17] Saltus probably shocked his essay readers more than his novel readers with statements like: "In history as in romance it is the shudder that tells. In menageries and zoos it is the wildest beast that obtains the best attention. . . . Contemporaneous crime is very commonplace."[18] His novels were never so wild, so fauve as they were advertised to be.

His characteristic essay tone depends on the shorter, the epigrammatic sentence or on turn of wit, balance, and pun; the following excerpt is a fair enough example:

> It is said of somebody somewhere that he became Poet Laureate because he lived on very good terms with his wife. That is certainly poetic. So also is the result. It constitutes a fine case of what a boulevardier might—if he thought of it——describe as *lauriat mediocritas*. Moreover, it shows, or seems to show, that connubial virtues are more estimable than literary sins. That is quite as it should be. But the converse of the proposition is equally true. Domestic difficulties are preferable to halting hexameters. The world is filled with good husbands. Good verse is more scant. For that matter, the better the verse the worse the husband. An ideal spouse would be both a perfect lover and a perfect poet. But no mere mortal has succeeded in being both, for any length of time at least; and very naturally too. The Muse is highly jealous. The task of serving two masters is nothing to having two mistresses on your hands.[19]

Irony pervades the passage. The prose, mannered but not unbearably so, is light; it does not take itself seriously; it amuses. The dig at queenly literary standards cuts, but the dig is good-humored. Only on occasion does today's reader feel the author twitting him, but a contemporary reader may have felt more powerfully twitted and resented it. The "domestic difficulties" and "halting hexameters" seem an amusing prose analogue to the heroic couplet; the caesura falls between two juxtaposed alliterative phrases. The contrast between the demands of wife and muse provide a perfect opportunity for frequent juxtaposition of balanced opposites. Saltus even risks "verse" and "worse" in the same sentence as deliberate comic strain. The short sentences, from four to seven words long, also pattern the light humor. The diction is colloquial and supple, the passage has flair, skill, wit. It may serve as an example of Saltus as popular essayist.

His worst excesses need not detain us. The following passage, the opening paragraphs of *The Imperial Orgy*, shows sufficient deterioration of the famous short sentence:

> Timur and Attila dwarf Ivan but not very much. In the fury with which Attila pounced on civilisation there is the impersonalty of a cyclone. Timur was a homicidal maniac with unlimited power and a limitless area in which to be homicidal. Where he passed he left pyramids of human heads and towers made of prisoners mixed with mortar. Where Attila passed he left nothing.
>
> Ivan turned cities into shambles and provinces into cemeteries. A cholera, corpses mounted about him. But death was the least of his gifts. He discovered Siberia. That was for later comers. For his immediate subjects he discovered something acuter. To them he was not cholera, he was providence. (1)

Perhaps it is not the short sentence become choppy, almost an affectation, that halts the reader's positive response to this passage but the frantic diction, the desperate reaching out for excess. The association of Ivan the Terrible with traditional monsters like Timur and Attila stretches the excess. Balance, contrast, surprise—the elements are the same—but not the aim. The objective of the sensational details—"pyramids of human heads," "towers made of prisoners mixed with mortar," "provinces into cemeteries"—is shock.

Yet Saltus could, as one critic put it, "squeeze an era into an epigram."[20] Aphorisms, so easily quoted and probably more characteristic of conversation than of the written word, came to be considered as a characteristic of Saltus. When he devoted the entire last chapter of his first work to a mere listing of wise sayings culled from the works of Balzac, without any sense that such a devotion was superfluous at best and superficial at worst, it seems likely that he was expressing an enjoyment of aphoristic wisdom common to an era when Shakespeare was so heavily rifled and when commonplace books, containing bits of wisdom, were popular.

Saltus could on occasion develop a passionate response as the excellent description of Tristrem Varick's nightmare shows. A brief paragraph is sufficient to display its hallucinatory power:

> He hurried on, and as he hurried he heard steps behind him, hurrying too. He turned his head; behind him was a woman run-

> ning, and who, as she ran, cast a shadow that was monstrous. In the glimpse that he caught of her he saw that she was bare of foot and that her breast was uncovered. Her skirt was tattered and her hair was loose. He turned again, the face was hideous. The eyes squinted, lustreless and opaque, the nose was squat, the chin retreated, the forehead was seamed with scars, and the mouth, that stretched to the ears, was extended with laughter. As she ran she took her teeth out one by one, replacing them with either hand. And still she laughed, a silent laughter, her thin lips distorted as though she mocked the world. (115)

Saltus renders the dread of capture in the classic dream of pursuit very well indeed. The face, not the body of the pursuer, has particularity and terror; the passage is, however, somewhat literary. It echoes a little the horrors that "Los Comprachicos" perpetrated on infants and children in Hugo's *l'Homme qui rit*. But the vivid, specific detail, "she took her teeth out one by one, replacing them with either hand," may derive from personal experience. The prose rhythms are also successful; Saltus moves to shorter sentences and never allows his syntax to become overcomplicated. Word repetitions reinforce the hurry, the running, the laughter. Supporting these repetitions are pronoun repetitions and parallel structures. He creates, finally, a figure parallel to Goya's black paintings. (Saltus' passionate appreciation of Goya is rare in American letters at any time and was especially so in the last century.)

A careful reader of Saltus may cull an adequate enough bouquet of rare and exotic words: "duscholia," "intussusception," "repercuted," "opopanax," "elenchicism." He finds eyes both "iserine" and "vesuvian" which may "horripilate" him or strike him as "utterly ramollescent." The hero who dreams of a honeymoon in "salmon, saffron, and smalt" may, caught in his dream, bump into an "engastrimuth." But the reader easily avoids the hero's fate because he usually moves amid a diction and a style that is lucid, easy, colloquial. When Saltus does step up his exoticism, he generally does so in set descriptions—of lovely young girls, of sunsets, and of other natural scenes. Set descriptions usually seem stuck in, and usually are; and the author, sensing their artificiality, often increases it by straining to offset it.

Surprise was an effect Saltus desired to achieve. If both humor and paradox are "the commonplace in fancy dress," the fancy dress, or surprise, could come in the rare word.[21] Frequently surprise meant the distortion of a commonplace as in the pun, "the infernal feminine," or as in the saying: "every silver lining has its cloud." Indispensable to epigram are concision, wit, and balance: "People marry out of curiosity and divorce out of optimism." "A man lives as long as he desires, and a woman as long as she is desirable." These last two examples are put into the mouth of the fictional daughter of Schopenhauer, Floriline; they are not spoken directly by Saltus who considered the series in which Floriline appears as ephemeral journalism.[22] Another example: "Manors used to make the man and Worth the woman."

Epigrams and witty turns of phrase also occur in the novels. At the very beginning of *The Perfume of Eros,* we encounter: "At his feet was an Ardebil rug which originally had cost a small fortune and now was worth a big one." From a *Collier's* column: "A lady who marries a second time does not deserve to have lost her first husband." The creations containing social comment are usually successful. "In a free country we are not allowed to sit on the grass" is still pointed. More extravagant and more suggestive as an index to upper-class manners is: "A bull-fight differs from an opera in many things, but particularly in this, that there may be exclamations, but there is no attempt at continuous conversation." Such is the world in which wives "would rather be dead than out of fashion."

Saltus, like Wilde, did not want to be commonplace. When he defends inconsistency of character, he does so on the ground that human beings act inconsistently and unexpectedly. Although the tenet can be defended as a form of Realist dogma, it also belongs to that of the 1890's; for, "to be interesting is admittedly, to say the opposite of what is expected."[23] Not surprisingly, a portion of the Saltus legend developed from reported conversation, from the public personality that supplied anecdotal copy to magazines and newspapers. Saltus was not only the subject of anecdotes but, as a frequent newspaper and magazine contributor, also the teller of them. Copy about him was, on the whole and expectedly, more flamboyant than copy by him. One well-known example:

Hostess—"Mr. Saltus, what character in fiction do you admire most?"

Saltus—"God."

Saltus as "Bourgeoisophobus" functions well. The examples given are effective social criticism: "Triviality is" indeed "the dandy's disguise" in them. Although Saltus cannot be called a "reformer," neither can he quite be called a social or a moral "subversive." We cannot say of him, as we can of Wilde in *The Importance of Being Earnest,* that "Whenever ordinary morality appears," he makes it seem ridiculous.[24]

For "ordinary morality" is the base of the Saltus contribution, as it is of most of Wilde's work. The particular ways in which both constructed and used pun, epigram, and paradox; their inversions; and their wit are related to one another and to the world of Baudelaire, Barbey d'Aurevilly, Joris Karl Huysmans, and others. The unexpected and the perverse become verbal masks through which criticism works; and which are also, of course, delights in themselves. As Wilde put it: "To expect the unexpected shows a thoroughly modern intellect." The perverse is better expressed by the French *à rebours* which became the title of the notorious "yellow book" ruinous to Dorian Gray, that unquestioned "breviary of the decadence," as Symons called it. Doing things *à rebours*—the wrong way round or against the grain, being and committing the perverse and the unexpected—was the way to experience the new thrill of discovery, of wickedness, of achievement, of delight in the self.

No "peacock phrases, glowing periods and verbal surprises" embellish every page of any single work by Edgar Saltus. His practice, by comparison with Wilde or with Huysmans, is more muted, soberer, less daring, less extravagant, less rich. While "yellow" came to be associated with the 1890's because of *The Yellow Book,* other colors also lighted up prose and painting: "Green had still many devotees"; Holbrook Jackson, the first chronicler of the movement in England, selects white as characteristic for its representation of innocence, for its "dash of the debauchee's love of virginity."[25] It appeared as silver, moonlight, starlight, ivory, alabaster, marble.

Critics have long associated purple with Saltus, probably because of the title *Imperial Purple,* or, because, as a contemporary reviewer put it, "Next to the purple cow of a celebrated poem the most purple thing we know of is the prose of Mr. Edgar Saltus."[26] In fact, he never uses purple with any meaning other than the traditional one of royalty. The color has no special place in his work, nor does any other color. However, like analogous contemporaries in England in France, he does like color in his prose. He never makes it an esthetic tool, a formal tactic which informs a whole work, as Stephen Crane does in *The Red Badge of Courage;* but he reflects the general sensitivity to colors both sharp and subtle. His association with purple tells us more about the critics who needed a figure to fill the role of wicked, irresistible dandy.

The ideal of style was an 1890's one that had its immediate origins in France—from the example of Flaubert, Baudelaire, and their successors. That art could be a religion and that judgments should be artistic rather than moral were part of the dandy's creed. That the total personality, its conversation and its dress, belonged to art was another *dandisme* tenet. Saltus, although an elegant man about town, never astounded the natives as Wilde and Gérard de Nerval did—notwithstanding the desperate effort of Sadakichi Hartmann to turn him into a sartorial offbeat: "I do not recall ever having seen him in anything but a dress suit." Hartmann sees him as a dandy of the Ward McAllister era, replete with "white socks, gloves, stovepipe, and walking stick."[27] Even if we accept Hartmann's report, the elegant dress he describes is conventional beside the sartorial show-stoppers of Wilde and de Nerval. But the concern for dress, like the concern for the polished word, was a concern for form in life and art.

Saltus was theoretically committed to the polishing and repolishing of prose. The evidence of his practice is, however, incomplete and indecisive. Of the six extant book-length manuscripts, four appear to be proofreaders' or printers' copies—*A Transaction in Hearts, Lords of the Ghostland, The Paliser Case, Imperial Orgy.* As a whole, the manuscripts are remarkably clean. Most are written in pencil in yellow, lined, legal-sized paper; but it is impossible to know whether any represents a first draft. Unfortunately, none of the earlier and better works exists in its several manuscript stages.

Charles Hanson Towne suggests a habit of composition which must have been as natural to Saltus as the laborious revision he advocated: "He made few alterations, for he wrote slowly; and once a sentence was committed to paper, there it remained." Towne also quotes Saltus as saying, "over and over on different occasions," that "Plasterers do not replaster, and bricklayers don't relay bricks. Why should weavers of words have to be constantly changing their blocks of sentences? God deliver me from the amateur in any art!"[28]

Other available manuscript material, short stories, essays, and poems are of little help. They show little or no additions, excisions, revisions; but, since we cannot be sure they are first drafts, we can only surmise Saltusian habits of composition. What abets the possibility that Saltus revised less than his legend has it is his remarkable productivity. If the dates that follow most of his novels are accepted as the beginning and end dates of composition, then Saltus wrote them with remarkable speed. Having written nine novels, one book of short stories, and four nonfiction books in nine years (1884-1895), it is not surprising that inclusive datings, when we have them, show Saltus writing a novel in two or three months, and one possibly in six months. During these years he was also the translator, editor, or compiler of three "serious" volumes and of five to nine potboiler volumes for P. F. Collier.

He must have worked at a furious pace. Even his acknowledged "first" work, *Imperial Purple,* appears to have been written in three months. Although there is no special merit to works written slowly over several years, the combination of Saltus' great quantitative production and his minor status as a writer suggest less devotion to revision than he had advocated. A less attractive version of polishing and repolishing could include Saltus' habit of using and reusing his own material, favorite lines or paragraphs (he took over the passage on Guerrita almost whole for the death of another matador, Frascuelo),[29] or whole plots (*The Paliser Case,* 1919, reworks *The Pace That Kills,* 1889). The generally unsuccessful nature of his repetitions, not the repetitions *per se,* become additional support for the picture of a writer burned out at forty, ravaging his earlier, more creative self for ideas.

The Saltus who rejected certain of the standard authors of his day—even as a boy he could not read Scott and "acquired a loathing for Carlyle that abides with me still"—admired others whom he found he could not in later life reread. Within the latter group he numbered Thackeray and even the Balzac who had inspired his first book. But Saltus was primarily a conscious carrier of post-Romantic theory, as his essays on fiction in *Love and Lore* adequately show. He never gave the fiction he discussed a name. He adopted neither the Realist nor the Naturalist label, but he does use a curious term which he seems to have coined himself. He refers in several places to "ornamental literature"—which may seem a perfect term for *fin-de-siècle* or "decadent" literature. Yet the contexts of the phrase suggest that "ornamental" is merely a synonym for imaginative literature—for fiction as distinct, for example, from history or from the essay.

Sometimes, however, it literally means ornate. In an essay called "Fashions in Poisons," reminiscent of the catalogues of des Esseintes in *A Rebours* and of the lesser sensuousness of Dorian Gray, Saltus writes: "In New York, a few years ago, a death occurred which a jewelled snake, resting for a second on a glass of champagne, is believed to have occasioned. The belief may be unfounded, yet the possibilities in it are splendidly ornate."[30] The subject and tone are perhaps closer to Max Beerbohm than to any other English "aesthete." In these two sentences is the Saltus that critic and public wanted. The jewelled snake may well remind the reader of the jewelled tortoise in *A Rebours* which dies, unable to bear its dazzling burden. The possibilities in such props are indeed "splendidly ornate." Ornate means here what we expect it to mean: the sensuous, the criminal, or the violent thrill or *frisson*.

The reader of today may need to be reminded that Flaubert authored the lush *Salammbô* as well as the realistic *Madame Bovary*. These two directions in Flaubert's fiction suggest a prose analogue to the image and the symbol in poetry. The image was hard, clear, precise, direct; the symbol, suggestive, shaded, indirect. Saltus, like Flaubert and other contemporaries, was attracted by both directions. He could be bare; he could be baroque. It is unlikely that he found these two styles antipodal or contradictory. The trajectory of his career shows him moving gradually toward the baroque, toward an impressionist prose that did not necessarily discard the short line. The brief analysis above of passages from *Incoul*, the lament for Guerrita, *Imperial Purple*, and *The Imperial Orgy* show a progressive reaching out for the superficially uncommon and extraordinary. Saltus became desperately afraid of the commonplace in himself and in his style. In a classic substitution of frenzy for matter, he adulterated his very real talent.

Put simply, style is a way of writing that we decide is a good one. In a nation divorced from its older tradition and unable to bring together its patrician practitioners with its upstart non-Easterners or middle- or lower-class practitioners, the Saltus effort was bound to remain incompletely realized or encouraged. Percival Pollard, discouraged and disgusted by Saltus' later "verbal vertigo," nonetheless concludes: "style, though it may claim a victim here and there, is still the saving salt of letters, the lack of which is so conspicuously our American defect."[31] The expatriate editor of the *Yellow Book*, Henry Harland, was, like Pollard, an admirer of Henry James. Wise enough to get James to contribute to his magazine's first issue, Harland said of him to a friend: "To me he seems the only master of considered prose we've got. Ah, but you're not mad about style as I am."[32]

Harland's remark is typical. For him and for his fellow upstarts English prose lacked the strength and precision of the French prose tradition. It had lapsed from its eighteenth-century high and was, as we now know, on the verge of a revolution. The writers of the 1890's were a crucial symptom of disturbance and dissatisfaction. They served the youth of the great poet William Butler Yeats and indirectly prepared for new sensibilities in the novel like Joyce, Woolf, and Lawrence. They did not so directly serve in the United States, for no single major writer came from its ranks. When the generation of the 1920's looked for leadership, it went directly to Europe, unaware that its primary attitudes had been discovered and discussed in a previous generation. Once more the contact between generations had been broken. Within the ranks of the pianissimo revolutionaries, younger writers could have found the same respect for the French tradition, the same respect for craft, and the same contempt for what Saltus called "the inflated proprieties of the Victorian regime."[33]

CHAPTER 5

Reflections on Literature

WALDEN

In swift and sudden dreams each night I greet
The host of friends that in my heart I bear;
I chat in paradox with Baudelaire,
I talk with Gautier of the obsolete–
My absinthe and de Musset's brandy meet:
And by some special favor here and there,
Now with Elaine and now with Guinevere,
I pass the day in some serene retreat.
Heine's malicious eyes have gazed in mine,
And I have sat at Leopardi's feet,
And once I heard the lute-strung songs divine
That Sappho and the Lesbian girls repeat,
But yet, what night have I not sought in vain
To meet and muse with Emerson again.[1]

WHAT SALTUS HAD TO SAY about other writers and contemporary literary issues shows he could locate major issues. His comments, more frequently casual than thorough, indicate a distinct awareness of current specialized literary concerns, of Realism, of Naturalism, of Symbolism, and of the larger, more general debates on art and morality, on art and economics, and on the crisis of craftsmanship in the novel. His discussions of writers, schools, audiences, and other literary subjects suggest the various levels of excellence that journalism can provide. They require a term less strict in its connotations than "literary criticism." The discussions are meant to delight, to irritate, to teach, and to earn money.

I *Other Writers*

The French Example

Edgar Saltus had only a peripheral interest in writing about other writers. *Balzac* (1884), his first book, was not a sign but a sport. Although he did, much later in life, devote essays to Victor Hugo and Oscar Wilde, he never again devoted an entire book to one author. He signals with this first book his primary involvement with French literature and his only secondary or tertiary involvement with English, American, Italian, and Russian literature. His attendance at Heidelberg and his admiration for Schopenhauer and von Hartmann had no apparent influence in awakening an interest in the literature of Germany. Within the first few years of the publication of *Balzac,* Saltus translated and introduced several stories by Balzac (*After Dinner Stories,* 1885) and by Théophile Gautier and Prosper Mérimée (*Tales Before Supper,* 1887). Later he translated Barbey d'Aurevilly (*Story Without A Name,* 1891) and had to face the charge that he had fabricated his author.[2]

Like his presentation of pessimism, his presentation of Balzac is reportorial and historical, not analytical and critical. Still, James Huneker was to credit Saltus with introducing Balzac to the wider American public—to the "Benighted States," as Saltus put it.[3] That the narrower American public was well aware of Balzac the reviews of Edgar's book show; primarily favorable, they accept the book as introductory and addressed specifically to readers unfamiliar with Balzac. Saltus praises Balzac's fiction for qualities his own was never to possess—its detail, breadth, social vision. He is also moved to admire Balzac's obsessive devotion to his creations and to his art. This "Benedictine of the actual" (the phrase is Henry James's) may have inspired in Saltus the desire to create a personal style. Although the Saltus style can hardly be said to derive from the Balzac style, Balzac's example was always there, as were the examples of several other French writers.

What Saltus did catch from Balzac was the trick of using the same characters in several novels. Some characters, like Mrs. Nicholas Manhattan, are never more than merely alluded to; others like Mr. and Mrs. Incoul and Viola Raritan, whom the reader of Saltus knows well, reappear as dinner guests or as opera neighbors in later novels. Only one character reappears and reappears—his ambiguous serio-comic alter-ego, the novelist, Alphabet Jones.

Balzac and Hugo were the undisputed giants of French literature by the time Saltus wrote about them. He had met Hugo and subsequently attended his funeral in 1885; it was a great and gaudy national event. He uses his essay on Hugo to insist on the autonomy of art, on the artist's ability to make "dreams that achieve immortality" because they become "more real than the children of men."[4] The power and seriousness of the essay—though it is more a discourse on time, art, and man than a criticism of Hugo's works—justify the author's feelings that it is the best bit of copy he had written in years.[5] His admiration for Hugo is in no way undermined by another essay which is more critical in its assertion that by writing "too much" Hugo allowed "the superficial and the trite" to enter his work.[6]

The bulk of Saltus' comments on other writers, on literary events and literary theories are scattered in his abundant newspaper and magazine articles, columns, essays, and novels. For awhile he had regular columns in *Once A Week* and *Collier's* (1893-1898), as well as frequent articles in the Sunday New York *Journal* (1896-c. 1900), and in other New York newspapers. He also contributed to *Cosmopolitan, Ainslee's, Munsey's, Smart Set, Harper's Bazar, Anti-Philistine,* and *The Wave,* a lengthy and striking testimony to the emergence of the mass and the little magazine—and a striking contradiction of the mysterious Saltus legend. The evidence suggests that Saltus chose and was accepted by mass more than by avant-garde media. He never wrote for *M'lle New York,* the little magazine edited by Vance Thompson and James Huneker which seems Saltus' more appropriate vehicle. He might have used his columns for extended literary comment but was probably expected or invited to use them for chit-chat about fashions, food, foibles, books, and personalities in high society or politics.

In those articles, columns, and essays, Saltus quotes, refers to, or comments about many other contemporary French writers. His knowledge is extensive, his estimates sometimes conventional and sometimes not. For Flaubert, Leconte de Lisle, Gautier, and Barbey d'Aurevilly, his admiration is unqualified. For others, like Baudelaire, Verlaine, Zola, it is qualified; for still others, like Mallarmé, it is highly qualified. His apparent unawareness of Rimbaud is not unusual. That he manages to bring Verlaine and Mallarmé into his popular *Collier's Weekly* columns is unusual, given the almost non-existent discussion of these writers even in "higher brow" magazines.[7]

Saltus appears to be both conservative and radical in his literary stands. When he discusses Realism and Naturalism, for example, he accepts fact as the common link between the two schools, but prefers Realism because in it "there is both fact and suggestion, whereas in the decadent naturalism of today the reader is offered but facts alone."[8] His position is "conservative" precisely at a time when he was enjoying a reputation as a literary radical. (He indicates elsewhere, as we shall see, that the novelist must transcend both schools.) Clearly he thinks of himself as a radical when he defends Balzac from charges of atheism and immorality. "Even today," he asserts, "there are many who look upon Balzac as a Sade and a Holbach rolled into one."[9] These positions suggest why Saltus, given his literary milieu, may be seen as both conservative and radical in his literary views.

Saltus' stricture against Naturalism did not prevent him from admiring Emile Zola. Though he does, on occasion, show some irritation with Zola's reportorial accumulations, or his exhibitionistic tendencies during the Dreyfus affair, he is absolute in his judgment that *l'Assommoir* is immortal. In 1885 he was even moved to defend Zola from the abuse then fashionable; for, as our proponent of pessimism puts it, the truths of Zola's descriptions show the perceptive reader the inherent pessimism of life.[10]

For Saltus, the state of poetry in France was more exciting than the state of the novel. He notes with remarkable accuracy France's transitional state after the death of Hugo in 1885, of Leconte de Lisle in 1894, of Verlaine in 1896, and of Mallarmé in 1898. The Symbolist group was internally split in 1900; indeed, the Parnassian view "seemed most secure in 1900."[11] Saltus was not, therefore, off-center in his predilection for the Parnassians, and was more than usually incisive in his diagnosis of the state of literary France as transitional.

To the Parnassian admirer, the Symbolists are dethroners of Hugo and of de Lisle, that "Goya of verse" and even "perhaps the most perfect poet of France."[12] Later, Saltus becomes phobic in his insistence that "Symbolism in literature is what bolshevism has become in life, a form of hydrophobia."[13] His insistence reads like the philistine's attack on whatever is new or modern—not because of its point of view, but because of its superficiality, its questionable equivalence of literary and political issues, and its easy dependence on current cliché to take his audience with him. The essay, posthumously published (1923), may not have been meant for publication. In any case, the later Saltus may be permitted to disagree with the earlier one.

"The symbolists, hungry for chaos, substituted delirium for calm and incoherence for clarity," the rabid Saltus says in his posthumously published essay. Another Saltus recalls with pleasure in the same essay the Verlaine of "the literary terror" as a brilliant conversationalist at the Café François Premier. Mallarmé does not fare so well: "he fell over backward into the incomprehensibleness of 'L'Après-midi d'un faune,' a poem that afterward fell deeper, into the gymnastics of a ballet."[14] The attack may be justified; Mallarmé *is* nearly incomprehensible. However, the source of the attack more likely lies in Saltus' age, illness, and nearly complete isolation from his literary milieu in his last years. At a time when the younger generation in Paris was celebrating in ballet the union of the arts, of dance, music, art and poetry, and "The Afternoon of a Faun" represented one such union, Saltus namecalls it "gymnastics." The tone is petulant; the content, shallow.

Five years earlier, in the summer of 1893, Saltus wrote from Paris a weekly column for the magazine *Once A Week*. In his August 19th column he reports the delightful anomaly of Paul Verlaine's announced candidacy for election to the Academy. Behold, "the man of all others who has been most indifferent, not alone to conventionalities but to laws, yields to vanity and knocks at the Academy door."[15] As Saltus plays with this anomaly, he tells us something of Verlaine's history. He credits Verlaine, not Mallarmé or Baudelaire, with "the foundation of that school of verse which a few years ago was called the Decadent, but which, from the initiate, has since received the more esoteric title of Symbolist."[16] He lists the delightfully outrageous postulate of the school, as he was to do again in 1898, that vowels have colors. Therefore, the poet's job is to group the shadings of words "prismatic with life." The subsequent image of "absolute

Bohemianism," replete with orgies, absinthe, sonnets (many of his own heros drink absinthe and write sonnets) and a hospital charity bed, reinforces the paradox of Verlaine's Academy candidacy. Finally, although Verlaine may be "better known by his eccentricities than his verse . . . the latter is exquisite." Whatever, then, Saltus' conservative literary views were in the twentieth century, we cannot say that he was totally unsympathetic to Symbolism in the 1890's.

If the frequently expressed judgment that modern literature finds its source in French literature is accepted, then Saltus showed some acumen in locating and publicizing it. He may not have seized on Baudelaire and Flaubert in the manner of modern critics; but he knew, as only Henry James knew better, that modern fiction owed its initiation and support to the abundant and varied French example. If, therefore, American writers and critics can no longer ignore French literature, then Saltus' efforts were among the first to make this state possible.

The American Example

American literature was hardly a mine for models. The two creators of an American literary language, Mark Twain and Walt Whitman, were very much there but probably too contemporaneous to serve as models. Saltus enjoyed Twain, did not mention Walt Whitman, and found himself most at home with Henry James.[17] He respected the older American writers: Emerson, Thoreau, Hawthorne, Poe.[18] He missed, like most of his contemporaries, the experience of Herman Melville and Emily Dickinson, but had a surfeit of best-sellers like F. Marion Crawford: how is it possible, he wondered, "for stupidity to be so verbose, and emptiness to be so heavy." His reponse to one popular author, Joaquin Miller, is generous. To the adult Edgar, the *Songs of the Sierra* despite their "occasionally . . . Byronic note," were "otherwise new"; and, to the adolescent Edgar, they seemed "splendid, and the legend of the minstrel, fighting Indians and the prairie fire while finding and fashioning his numbers, superb."[19] Saltus embraced, like millions of other boys, adventures with a specific Western American color. He was not shy about saying so years later when press agents considered exotic purple his distinctive color.

In an era that loved to search literature for wise and quotable sayings, the statement that a complete collection of Balzac's "theories and teaching would be as impossible as an arrangement of Emerson's best thoughts" is a compliment.[20] *Balzac* and the *Philosophy of Disenchantment* allude to Emerson sufficiently to show that Saltus had read him recently and with intensity. His use of Emerson is partially pragmatic, for allusions to America's only philosopher would help his audience to understand Schopenhauer, who becomes an "Emerson in black." He places him with seers he admires, with the Hugos rather than the Hegels.[21] Saltus' reverence has some justification, for his fellow American had carried far the romantic axiom of self-realization which underlies the Decadent or Symbolist point of view and still governs our ideals of human behavior. Saltus was to tell James Huneker that he and Emerson were his only American prophets;[22] and, in his sonnet dedicated to Emerson, first called "Walden" and then "A Memory," he bends his knee to the prophet.

Saltus shows no recognition that his admiration of Poe might jar with his admiration of Emerson. We cannot, however, make too much of the casual references which make up Saltus' views of his compatriot writers. Poe, like Baudelaire, serves his pessimistic hobby-horse. He is also an example of the persecuted artist still on trial even after his death.[23] In Poe, Saltus presents us with the by now familiar figure of the *poète maudit.* (Whitman ignored that role.) Saltus may well have fixed his attitude toward Poe through the French admiration for him; he would not be the first American to do so. He is primarily interested in the special horrors and plots of Poe's short stories—stories his own practice surely learned from.

It was easy for Saltus to pick the best contemporary American novelist, Henry James; and his regard for the novelist is unqualified. In his *Philosophy of Disenchantment* (1885), he praises *The Portrait of a Lady* (1881), connecting what he construes as its inner pessimism with the new Realism. His connection of James with European writers like George Eliot, Turgenev, and Stendhal is not accidental, although the dedication of *Mary Magdalen* (1890) to him does seem so, since it is a historical novel. In an 1897 *Collier's* column Saltus beautifully supports James's work for his common reader: "It is not good and artistic in spots, it is good and artistic all over. There is not today anyone, anywhere, who writes as he does. He is the great master of English prose."[24]

Saltus writes without any deep sense of connection with American or British literary tradition. Nevertheless, like two other contemporaries, James Gibbons Huneker and Percival Pollard, Saltus did not hesitate to choose James emphatically as the best American novelist. Huneker and Pollard spoke louder and longer for James, but all three championed him prior to the so-called James revival of the twentieth century, as did the older, more established William Dean Howells.

The poets whom Saltus knew form a middle generation between poets of the "genteel tradition" and those of the radical early twentieth-century tradition. They fall between poets like E. C. Stedman and R. W. Gilder and Ezra Pound and T. S. Eliot. R. H. Stoddard, a member of the earlier tradition, found Swinburne "exceedingly narrow, obscure, and tedious"; for Edgar and his friends, his work was new and exciting. For the succeeding generation, it was everything poetry ought not to be, as T. E. Hulme strongly indicates: "I think that there is an increasing proportion of people who simply can't stand Swinburne."[25]

Most of Edgar's contemporaries, men like Edgar Fawcett, Francis Saltus, Owen Meredith, wrote easily and in the Victorian lyric tradition. Music was generally extravagantly more central than sense in their poetry, and within such a context Whitman was an outsider, unless he be admitted, as he very likely was, as a bohemian. Saltus never claimed major or powerful minor status for his poet-friends, but they constituted his American literary circle. Edgar's friends chafed within the establishment, but they were still members of it. Gifted, cultivated, fluent, charming, they vanished from critical memory almost as quickly as some of them composed. A young writer could not learn from them what he needed to know. Poetry was not to be first-rate in America, except for the isolated examples of Walt Whitman and Emily Dickinson, until the twentieth century.

The English Example

Neither Oscar Wilde nor Edgar Saltus published in the little magazines associated with the esthetic movement of the 1890's, although both were considered major figures in the movement in their respective countries. They had met at Delmonico's during Wilde's first American tour in 1882 when both were in their late twenties. They met again in London in 1890 and probably on other unrecorded occasions. In a letter to Saltus, Wilde found one Saltus work, "so pessimistic, so poisonous and so perfect."[26] The adjectives and the alliteration must have pleased the American epigrammatist and paradoxist whose loyalty to Wilde we have no reason to question even after Wilde's trial in April, 1895, which American editors left unrecorded in their periodicals.[27] Saltus did not, however, speak out for Wilde at this crucial juncture; within the context that omission is not surprising, though perhaps not justifiable. His public appreciation of Wilde occurs in the twentieth century, primarily through a memoir solicited by Richard Le Gallienne.

In *Oscar Wilde: An Idler's Impression*, published in 1917, Saltus presents through a series of anecdotal reminiscences his version of the sacred terror that authentic art produces. In *Salomé,* Wilde produced that terror which at other times Wilde, Saltus, and the French call the shudder or *frisson.* Morality has nothing to do with authentic art unless the writer cares to cultivate "the art of never displeasing." Oscar Wilde, Saltus concludes, "lacked that art and I can think of no better epitaph for him."[28]

The splendid epitaph did not mean Saltus could not consider Wilde "a third rate poet who occasionally rose to the second class but not once to the first." Saltus frequently astonishes by his unembarrassed, direct appraisals—by his honesty within what would be normally only encomium. He praises in Wilde what was praised in himself, in his brother, in James Huneker, and in so many other writers of the day, the brilliance of his conversation: "He talked infinitely better than he wrote."[29] The oral splendor of the era was not limited to bohemians and esthetes; Mark Twain and other Western Americans contributed to it from another direction.

Saltus also had occasion to praise the work of Aubrey Beardsley and Francis Thompson. But the kinship between English and American writers of the 1890's may owe more to their common French source than to their own interrelationship, even for a writer like Henry Harland who was so closely connected with the English esthetes. Saltus probably knew Harland, godson of the conservative E. C. Stedman, and editor of the *Yellow Book,* for both belonged to a period when most literary men were still interrelated by family and class. Another member of the Anglo-American avant-garde, Frank Harris, felt that a visit to New York without meeting Saltus would be like a visit to "Egypt without seeing the Sphinx."[30]

Out of his involvement with other writers past and present Saltus created what literary roots he had. He never spoke in terms of originality; he spoke only of assimilation when he considered the sources of an artist's powers. "Ability," he had written in his last extant notebook (c. 1896-c. 1913), "is the power of assimilation. Only a fool imagines he invents." In his earliest notebook (c. 1883-c. 1895) he noted, "Baudelaire said when I want an idea I take a good one and look at it crooked."[31] Saltus' search was ravenous, but his digestion was not thorough. As we have noted, only a sampling of his literary criticism can be considered more than journalistic. When he turns, however, from specific writers to a general consideration of the false morality and standards which informed most discussions of the novel in his day, the quality of his criticism is more passionate and more thorough.

II *"The Age Demanded . . ."*

To educate and thereby to create an adequate audience were major functions of nineteenth-century criticism. The new and larger reading public needed to be trained if letters were not to capitulate wholly to vapidity or to, as Saltus put it, "pastorals and fairy-tales." The great middle class, which had come into its own, forced a rebuttal to its conception—or to its spokesmen's conception—of morality in fiction, to its elaborate preconceptions of how a novel ought to instruct and be constructed. Henry James wrote "The Art of Fiction" to refute the binding moral and artistic strictures of Walter Besant, a contemporary English critic. In books, as well as in magazine and newspaper articles, Edgar Saltus frequently wrote with strength and eloquence on behalf of higher standards in fiction and of a less constricting conception of morality in literature.

Like Henry James, Walter Blackburn Harte, and many other writers who wrote against the popular grain, Saltus attacked what Harte called "the great American picket fence of respectability."[32] The fence was built with commercialism, for pseudo-morality seemed a comfortable ally of profits. In an effective parody, Saltus describes current literary trends in stock market vocabulary: "the pseudo-historical novel is firm. . . . Futures in prime western stories are active and higher. Dialect messes in tubs, fresh or fancy, slack. . . . In dressed essays no sales reported. Boer articles heavy. Magazine barrels unchanged." Outdoing even pseudo-history and surface local color are cookbooks, fashion plates, Bradstreet ratings, encyclopedias, and "ready references of every kind. These, together with little treatises on how to behave, how to succeed, how to get along without a doctor, how to know enough to come in when it rains are the grist in the American mill." Saltus suggests that the literary industry ought to create its own trust, "a monopoly of authors," with the power to issue scrip and convertible bonds. His ironic analogy concludes with his expectation that the national literary industry will achieve maximum efficiency and so force the public to "take more stock" in its authors than it does now.[33]

Saltus refuses the conclusion that condones crimes against art "on the ground that they possess the indorsement of public opinion." The artist who accepts this conclusion and caters to public stupidity instead of delivering his "fallen people" is corrupt. Thus Saltus reserves some of his sharpest criticism for the novelist who tries to please and who tries to succeed in a literary industry properly described in stock-market vocabulary and improperly aspiring to the condition of the trust—aspiring, in effect, to parallel the morality and structure of post-Civil War industry. He invokes his favorite Epictetus to support one of his favorite, frequently repeated axioms: "In the art of pleasing is the whole secret of mediocrity." Less expected is his invocation of Mark Twain, who had his share of flirtations and false encounters with money-making schemes: " 'Be good and you will be lonesome,' added Mark Twain, who must have had the dismal future of contemporary novelists in view."[34]

The concept of the isolation of the artist, developed in the Romantic period (and still active in our own), is coupled by Saltus with the inadequacy of the artist's audience. The appeal for higher standards in writers in this old debate always implicitly if not explicitly means an equal appeal for a perceptive audience. When one of Saltus' point-of-view characters says that "the majority is always cocksure and dead wrong,"[35] and another that he will give up writing the day he pleases everyone, the reader recognizes the Romantic locus of their attitudes. But their author wanted, as what writer does not, Stendhal's "happy few" or Milton's "fit audience though few." It was this minimal audience in its sociological sense (in its absolute sense it may never be accessible to measurement) that the United States lacked. So the good writer—like many of our nineteenth-century writers, Poe, Hawthorne, Melville, Dickinson, James—was the lonesome writer.

The only member of the audience frequently particularized is the "Young Person" or the "Young Girl," from the *jeune fille* in the French discussions of the problem. Saltus denies that the lack of felt life in our novels is due to the "Young Person," "for ignorance has never preserved a virtue yet."[36] Although Saltus and Howells are, in the fundamental sense, on the same side of the critical fence, Howells is willing to see the Young Girl's invocation by critics as a sign of better manners in fiction rather than as an evasion or as a sign of prudery. Howells proposed within his advocacy of Realism that "the large, cheerful average of health and success and happy life" was peculiarly American. He did agree that death and disease occurred in America, but he was stopped by his nationalist axiom (even Herman Melville preferred a mediocre American work to a first-rate English one) that American literature must be peculiarly American. It led the genial Socialist to suggest, in what became an unfair tag line, that our novelists are wise to "concern themselves with the more smiling aspects of life, which are the more American." Caught in a prescriptive criticism based on a questionable premise, Howells nearly vitiated his support of "fidelity to experience and probability of motive." He could foresee that Realism might one day become false and even perish, "when it heaps up facts merely, and maps life instead of picturing it"; but he could not find a place for the passion of love in American literature.

Around the portrayal of love the major issues—standards, audience, morality—forcibly collide. Saltus opposes the French and the Russian schools of fiction to the New England ethos. In a

Collier's column noting the death of Harriet Beecher Stowe, Saltus attributes her vicious attack on Byron's private life and much else in her career to her early surroundings: "hard, illiberal, rarefied and hard with hardness, illiberal with that illiberality which was peculiar to New England."[37] Thus, the novel may contain murder and villainy but love "must be treated from the Puritan stand-point." Thus, a Boston audience may sit through a performance of *Oedipus* and applaud a play whose "central situation is barely mentionable in ordinary speech"; and no one calls Sophocles immoral. The reader, suffering from an indigestion of "whipped cream and filigrees," wants better food. Saltus offers, characteristically, truffles, not steak.

His conception of a truer treatment of love is certainly not the Howells version of love. The "actualistic" school—which Saltus defends and which is, in "Saltus on Erotic Literature" (1894), a synonym for Realism—does not eliminate that "most powerful of all human emotions." To Saltus, "every healthy man and woman has feelings relating to the opposite sex that cannot be repressed." But the novels of Howells make the reader exclaim, " 'Why, I cannot make love in that cold-blooded way. I have stronger, intenser feelings that are not even hinted at here. If this be a truthful picture of human affliction and virile love-making, then I am a monster'." Saltus uses the venerable axiom that art must hold a mirror up to nature. Howells, he holds, does not; the "actualistic" school does; and "All in art that comes closest to nature will last." This axiom is hardly the one that represents modern fiction, poetry, or art; but it is a principle that could and did act as a radical touchstone to indicate the mediocrity of American fiction. Saltus knew the score and stated it bluntly: "Our only novelists of any pretensions are Howells and James and they are not read."[38]

Realists from Balzac, Flaubert, and Hugo to Zola are not "printed panders to depraved passions"—nor are they examples of eroticism or erotic literature.[39] The terms are analogues of today's "pornographic" and "pornography." They reflect the power and the extent of middle-class morality. Howells insisted that there are other passions beside love, a position that the post-Freudian generation may be delighted to embrace; but the problem, as Saltus pointed out, was the appalling general "poverty of thought" in the contemporary novel. That poverty was enough "to make the rest of us tear out our hair in the agony of the anguish of the resulting boredom." In what is probably his sharpest expression of anger and agony over the omissions and the shallowness of American fiction, Saltus asks the public to see what it distorts into a virtue:

> Life is not made up of scenery, platitudes and bad grammar. Life is made up of delight and torture, greed and hate, love and indifference, passion and despair. It is made up of emotions, not pap, and it is pap that we get for our money. By way of compensation, we are enabled to regard ourselves as a moral people. It is a pity that, as a people, we cannot look in a glass. It would break—that glass would. Yet, though we cannot look in it, others have held it up.[40]

There are, for Saltus, finally but two classes of fiction—"stories which are well-written and stories which are not." This position is probably his true one. He is, however, willing to present on occasion a compromise position: "An author may handle any topic, however *scabreux*, provided that he seeks less to entertain than to instruct."[41] But Saltus has too many other times played down or ignored instruction as an aim of the novel for the reader to take him entirely at his word.

Saltus as essayist prefers hints to hammers; and although he probably judged Naturalism to be the hammer of his day, he was neither its militant detractor nor defender. Considering both Romanticism and Naturalism as limited in appeal, Saltus expects and awaits "some hero of letters" who "will brush them both aside" in the interests of the future novel. In a farsighted list, Saltus predicts such a novel will have profited by the study of crowds as well as of "the unit," of "the multiplicity of the ego, the variable influence of surroundings, the change of views that ensue." It will have searched for "the invisible cause, the coordination of contradictories, the inevitable deduced from chance," from whatever lies behind the visible act.[42]

Saltus, in effect, awaits a novelist who will use and transcend both Romanticism and Naturalism. He ends his essay on "The Future of Fiction" with a buoyant sense of the variety and the excitement of the new fiction that is to come; and he evinces no fear of the unknown, or the new. "The corpse still warm," Romanticism, and the "silk stocking filled with mud," Naturalism, are irrelevant to him beside specific novelists like Dostoevsky, Flaubert, and Eliot who show the "disinterestedness, charity, and forgiveness of sin" which Saltus associates with the moral.[43] He chooses, as he should, the specific novel and novelist over the school or movement.

When he turns to the future of American literature, the cosmopolitan Saltus surprises us by contrasting the nation's "grandly manifest" social, political, and commercial qualities with its not so "grandly manifest" fiction. In a rare moment, even Saltus invokes a sense of national destiny to convince his readers that literature must change. He must suggest that national grandeur is incomplete without literary grandeur. He declines to lament over the American lack of tradition, for time "will fill that gap unprompted."[44]

Compare Saltus with an avant-garde contemporary, Walter Blackburn Harte, a well-known little magazine editor and writer who makes no concession at all to nationalist sentiment in his attempt to find out "Why American Novels are Flabby." In this essay, Harte believes the writer must go against the grain of his society because it encourages him to display only "the colourless optimism, the unreal complacence and cheery acceptance of every whitewashed iniquity, or moral sore of organised society." Our "conscience of bigotry and ignorance . . . overshadowed by the lingering gloom of Puritanism" makes the nurturing, development, and recognition of genius almost impossible both here and in England.[45] Hence Harte must also turn his reader to French and Russian models.

Harte's radical, spirited essay insists that "The flourishing commercial industries of the promoters of morality demand the complete suppression of *genius* as an intrinsic quality of intellect in America." For Americans equate genius with immorality; and, if they are berated for their lack of literature, they reply: " 'Oh, but we are moral!!' " Harte had no respect for popular taste and no illusion that habit and custom constitute morality: "Greed and the Pander always play the moral card."[46] Saltus had found the same ironic alliance between commerce and the champions of morals. He did, however, allow himself to await "the great American novel," which could fuse contrary elements, the Slav and the Latin, thinking and feeling, "the terrible and the ridiculous, ferocity and mirth."[47]

The brief suggestion is an interesting one. To see the American character as a mixture of extremes has more sanction in the violent political and economic history of the period than to see it as genial, contained, equable. We may be overaware of the dangers that surround any attempt to define a national character; it would be difficult to be underaware of younger fiction writers who courted extremes of melodrama, of motivation, and setting—and belied the Howells vision of American life. The sharp examples are Frank Norris, Jack London, Stephen Crane, Theodore Dreiser.

Saltus knew from his own experience how oversimplified current critical reception could be. For an interview written in 1891 he reviewed the reception of his first four novels.[48] When, he reports, he chose situations from real life in *Mr. Incoul's Misadventure* and in *Tristrem Varick,* he was reviled, denounced as immoral—but his books sold. In *Eden* he tried romance. His perplexity remained, for he was praised but let alone. In his next novel, *A Transaction in Hearts,* he mixed the real and the fictitious, "the complex and the simple," even made the heroine indifferent to the attentions of her clergyman brother-in-law and "left the clergyman horrified at himself." The "chorus of abuse" which followed made the "secret of selling and of pleasing . . . as remote as before." Certain that his literary ethics were upright, Saltus could conclude only that his failure was "due to the fact that the logic of his ethics was left more to the imagination than to the last page. It was suggested, not hammered in." Saltus finally returns to his view that "a writer who respects his pen writes what he must and not what he might" and inevitably places himself against public opinion. Such is the frustrating personal parable of the writer-critic-audience relationship.

Only the rare writer can be better than his audience or his milieu. The probability is that unless the artist is a genius in that word's extreme Romantic sense he will not dominate his context. The middle-order figure who needs and wants a relationship with his audience but cannot make one has his dilemma and his struggle. Such a figure would probably find it hard to prosper as *poète maudit* or expatriate, the two main postures open to the disaffected writer of the later nineteenth century. The *poète maudit* in his posture of open rebellion had his difficulties, but the century forced the posture and made it workable. The examples of Poe and Baudelaire were there. The expatriate examples of Byron and James were also there. Saltus, though he traveled frequently between Europe and the United States, chose neither type of exile. The alternatives probably did not exist for our middle-order figure who tried instead to woo his audience—although he knew his courtship was doomed.

CHAPTER *6*

Crime and Love: Historian and Amorist

"J'oserais affirmer, sans crainte d'être dementi, que Byron et de Sade (je demande pardon du rapprochement) ont peut-être été les deux plus grands inspirateurs de nos modernes, l'un affiche et visible, l'autre clandestin—pas trop clandestin."

SAINTE-BEUVE, 1843

In history as in romance it is the shudder that tells.

"Human Hyenas"

EDGAR SALTUS' excessive fondness for antithesis, contradiction, and paradox is not merely a matter of style. It is an expression of his fundamental way of seeing and organizing experience. His obsession with Ares, with crime, violence, and duplicity is as great as his obsession with Aphrodite and Eros. He searches history voraciously for examples of both. The underside of the moon was always there for the Romantics to wonder about, to try to see, if not to explain. A good deal of nineteenth-century literature exhibited the thematic complex of incest, sacrilege and crime or death. Shelley found incest, "like many other incorrect things, a very poetical circumstance." The thirst for an unrealizable or criminal love was frequent. De Quincey wrote on "Murder as One of the Fine Arts." Satan became a hero. These partial examples of the revolution in sensibility we call Romantic, a term "elusive, tiresome, indispensable,"[1] did not disappear when what we call Decadent literature succeeded what we call Romantic literature. It has not yet disappeared, for the basic sensibility of the twentieth century is still Romantic.

I *Rome and Russia*

The "shudder that tells" in history and in romance is the one that brings pain and pleasure together. It is the shudder that responds to the similar point of ecstasy in the horrible and the sublime. The extremes that Hugo brings together in the disfigured Gwynplaine and in the beautiful, blind Dea in *l'Homme qui rit* are familially related to Saltusian monsters and beauties, and to many more recent grotesques created by Sherwood Anderson, William Faulkner, or Carson McCullers.

But Saltus' first foray into history for Fauvist examples of human life that his own time may not have provided is more spectacle than shudder. *Mary Magdalen* (1891) purportedly originated in a conversation with Oscar Wilde in which both Saltus and Wilde agreed to write a work containing the figure of Salome; their common inspiration was Flaubert's *Hérodias*.[2] But the lush opening descriptions, the brilliant chariot race and the succeeding dance of Salome soon give way to an indirect examination of the doctrines of the biblical Jesus through Mary's conversion and her loyalty to Jesus until his crucifixion and resurrection. Where Mary, by her conversion, could serve as the character vehicle for doctrine, she functions instead as a shadowy figure. Saltus did give to the well-known biblical story an unexpected twist; he has Judas develop a passion for Mary which is unreturned even when he bribes her with his threat of "Love me or I turn the Master in." The book is not quite novel and not quite history. The descriptions suggest *Imperial Purple*, also finished in 1891 although published in 1892. The long digression by Mary's old nurse, Sephorah, based on "Assyrian annals and Egyptian lore" suggests *The Lords of the Ghostland* (1907). The sudden lengthy discourse on other versions of creation belongs to the essay not to the novel. Unsure of novelistic techniques, Saltus wisely turned to history as essay in *Imperial Purple* and *The Imperial Orgy*.

Saltus' fascination with special aspects of man's recorded memory, its kings, gods, and goddesses, never drowned his interest in contemporary events. To say, as critics so frequently have said, that an interest in the past is an escape is simplistic. The sensibility involved is more complicated, for Flaubert wrote *Madame Bovary*, as well as *Salammbô* and *The Temptation of Saint Anthony*. Escapism is evasion, and as such is not the peculiar province of time past or time present. If Saltus evades, he evades in both times. It is much more likely that the nature of his interest in the past parallels his interest in the present.

In *Imperial Purple* Saltus presents a series of impressions of Roman leaders from Caesar to Heliogabalus. The sources are traditional—Suetonius, Tacitus, Juvenal, Lampridius. The point of view tends to get lost in the gleaming splendor of fabrics, jewels, crimes. The collocation of the horrible and the sublime seems to be the point of view: the lives of the bloodthirsty emperors "are horrible, yet analyze the horrible and you find the sublime." The author's fascination with Rome is very much a fascination with the complexity of urban life; for the Rome of Caesar was "a Rome quite like London—one that was choked with mystery, with gold and curious crime." Much later in the work Saltus defines religion as "purely political," and, in the Roman world, connected with civic religiosity and a concept of immortality centered in descendants rather than in a personal afterlife. Such underpinnings of the more traditional matter of history consort with "No man, said a thinker, is wholly base. Caracalla was. He had not a taste; not a vice, even, which was not washed and rewashed in blood."[3]

The work ends with the defeat of the ancient empire by Christianity, metaphorically rendered: "Where the thunderbolt had gleamed, a crucifix stood. On the shoulders of a prelate was the purple that had dazzled the world."[4] Although prelate supplants emperor, the author's central concern is still with the man at the top of the power pyramid. In the long list of caesars between Caesar and Heliogabalus, there are greater and lesser emperors, as well as a variety of motives, purposes, and characters; there is light and shadow and a sense of development and change. What one observer calls "the striking absence of moralizing on past events" may permit us to notice and even to consider the proposition that Saltus merits a layman's place beside historians like Henry Charles Lea.[5] Certainly Saltus' layman's fascination with the rise and fall of empires and the power of economic forces is not surprising in the environment that produced the historical theories of Brooks Adams and Henry Adams and a history that James Harvey Robinson could justifiably call "new."

But truth is not Saltus' object; his object is the *frisson,* the shudder, the thrill. It is not even so much that he sees the mass of mankind under the control of caesars; he is not, in fact, presenting a theory of history. His interest is in the spectacular individual, an interest common to the nineteenth century. The data for the so-called ordinary individual did not become a part of the historian's studied province until the turn of the century, and his history remains difficult for lack of primary data. In a sense, Saltus perfected a special genre, one more related to the familiar essay of the nineteenth century than to any other genre —and one dead today.

Amid the riches of Roman history Saltus could also immerse himself in points of view about politics, religion, and morality that were more various and more direct, probably more honest, than he could find in his daily newspaper. In such immersion in the past, a writer might paradoxically be freer to learn and to comment on present-day politics and history than if he were to stay with his own time and place. Actually the comparable figures in his own time the captains of industry like James Fisk, Jay Gould, Andrew Carnegie, James J. Hill, E. H. Harriman, John D. Rockefeller, John Jacob Astor—were still alive and not quite ready to have their remarkable heads stuck on poles for the populace to learn from, to be terrorized and amused by. The Saltus who saw love and lucre as the motivating forces of history knew what industrial geniuses could amass in his time and at what cost and without purple robes. The contemporary counterparts of the caesars and the czars were these titans, not the United States presidents or the enfeebled European royalty. This comparison shows that an appreciation of the spectacular individual's role in history is not entirely naïve.

Rome's essentially military and administrative economy—"she consumed, she did not produce"—may also have invited comparison with the United States. The United States may have seemed to Saltus as intellectually dependent as Rome; what Rome had of "religion, literature, art, philosophy, luxury and corruption, everything had come from abroad."[6] Saltus was also to invite comparison between ancient Rome and modern Russia, but modern Russia did not invite much comparison with the United States.

Imperial Purple was Saltus' greatest success. Critics consistently chose it as his masterpiece. Nonetheless its status is bound to suffer in an era little attracted by history decked out as impressionist essay. If we discount, as it is fair to do, the volumes on Germany, India, and other nations done as potboilers for P. F. Collier, then Saltus' next venture into history occurs twenty-eight years later in 1920. In that year before his death, Saltus pieced together, reworked, and expanded a series of articles on the Russian czars from Ivan the Terrible to Nicholas "the Last" under the title, *The Imperial Orgy*. His original title, *Imperial Sables*, is even more obviously an attempt to recall and to match his earlier success. Purples and sables give way to an orgy of blood; history gives way to the movie spectacular in which millions of extras die as the ruthless king indulges and satisfies his lust for blood. As an older man, Saltus saw only blood at the center of history; the czars were "haematomaniacs." In a work which must have been motivated by the present—World War I, the Russian Revolution and the end of the czars—Saltus becomes shrill and remote.

He thought he had found a parallel to the worst excesses of the caesars of Rome: "The history of Russia is an expurgated edition of that of Rome." Insane as he finds both those who perpetrate and accept atrocity, Saltus still thrills to the specialness of madness. Perhaps, he muses, Ivan was mad; for "it is only the mad who are delivered from the commonplace." Some lines are embarrasing: "Peter was a gorilla with brains"; or "Nihilism and bolshevism differ, but only in spelling." Peter was the original bolshevist, Catherine the Great was "a tyrant and a lesbian who passed through history dripping with blood and exhaling the perfume of Eros" and the last Nicholas, a man "whose intelligence even Victoria regarded as limited."[7]

The older Saltus still had a good deal of blood in him, for he was not afraid to call the United States an autocracy: "Kant, in defining liberty, said that it consists in obeying those laws only to which we have given our assent. In any autocracy, particularly in the United States, where one has all the forms of liberty and none of the substance, assent is implied. Under the tsars and under the Caesars, even the forms were lacking."[8]

Such sudden sharp thrusts are typical of Saltus. By the end of the work Saltus has even partially shifted his position on Bolshevism. The erroneous connection of Nihilism with Bolshevism seems pejorative until the line: "Nihilism, mother of Bolshevism, came, as her daughter came, from Germany." Although Saltus was a rabid anti-German during World War I, he owed his intellectual birth to German philosophy. Hence Bolshevism and Nihilism are not entirely pejorative to him. In his final evaluation, his belief that Bolshevism might be the agent for the world's refurbishing is curiously supported by his surface theosophy. "Sovietism" seems to have come upon the earth "as a supernormal phenomenon, propelled from planes where events are marshalled, and designed to be the obstetricy of universal palingenesis."[9]

The very cloudy writing gets cloudier in these last paragraphs. When Saltus says "Scepticism is history's bedfellow," he is permitting himself to doubt the victory and durability of any system. He recalls the efforts of Greece, Rome, and France to sustain their greater, their freer moments; and he doubts that Russia will ultimately have any better luck than they, especially since the true goal of sovietism is "slavery and rationed misery." Saltus cannot resist a final suggestion that great things may come from Russia although he defers, at the very end, to Karma who "alone can tell."

Saltus tries, therefore, to have it both ways. His training keeps him from a thorough acquiescence in hysterical, ignorant anti-Bolshevism, but it is not sufficient to move him to precise research into and statement about current Russian history. Although, like most Americans of the time, he was strongly anti-czarist, he never joined the radical Americans who saw in the revolution the beginnings of a great Socialist future. He allows himself only the metaphoric formulation that simooms sweeps the desert man must cross before he reaches his paradise. Bolshevism, we take it, is one of the simooms on the way.

Later generations have not found that "haematomania" needs dressing up. Perhaps Saltus did place "his finger straight upon [the] combustible elements" of whatever he touched. Perhaps he was once "the prince of literary incendiaries."[10] Except for penetrating gleams that recall the younger Saltus, *The Imperial*

Orgy is like the superlatives of a movie advertisement—they cancel one another out. Unlike *Imperial Purple, The Imperial Orgy* has no variety of tone or value. Saltus had put his finger on the original political event of the war years, but what he did with it can only strike a contemporary as pseudo-history or poster art.

II *Crime, War and Empire*

His interest in Rome and Russia is also an interest in crime. War as organized crime, or as the chronic condition of mankind, fascinated Saltus as much as any other kind of crime. Whatever squeamishness he may have had did not keep him from seeing at least one Sing-Sing electrocution, visiting the morgue, reporting a famous four-week murder trial, or reporting on suicides or miscarriages of justice in murder trials.[11] His reportorial instinct in his *Once A Week,* in his *Collier's* columns, in his Sunday articles for the New York *Journal,* and in his magazine articles during the 1890's is strong. The necessities of the job do not entirely explain such forays; they also interested him.

He may even have used one item in a novel. In a Parisian trial the lone hold-out juror later turns out to be the murderer. In the trial in *The Paliser Case,* the hold-out juror is Angelo Cara, who will not judge the accused guilty because he is himself the murderer of his daughter's seducer, Monty Paliser. The refrigerated face in the morgue precipitates a reminiscence of the Paris morgue and a comparison of our suicide mores with those of the Hindus, Buddhists, Greeks, and Romans, none of whom assume that suicide is either insane or cowardly. Or, Saltus refers to Pierre Janet, to his exploration of "the tenebrous borderlands" where obsessions originate, and to his experiments which go "beneath the frontiers of the understanding" to "the lost lands of subconsciousness."[12]

These examples indicate Saltus' constant need to present the odd and the offbeat to his readers—or is it only a need to present the newsworthy? Nevertheless, very few journalists would have examined in 1898 the relative cruelty of guillotining, electrocution, and hanging as modes of capital punishment. When Saltus decides the guillotine is the cruelest because the severed head "retains its faculties for at least an hour" after decapitation, and therefore recommends it for anarchists, is his recommendation meant seriously or is he twitting his reader? Does he really find the corrida a "revolting spectacle" or is he adopting the common American view so that he can then say, as he does, that electrocution is an even more revolting spectacle?[13] He was certainly very much affected by the electrocution he saw and by the ritual surrounding it. He may have put his head in a pillow in his later years, but there is no evidence to suggest that it was there during the 1880's and 1890's.

To have developed with depth and detail the thesis that history and crime are nearly synonymous would indeed have been an event in the America of the 1890's. Unfortunately, Saltus' interest in crime and society materializes more in asides or undeveloped remarks than in genuine polemic. He asserts, for example, in "Human Hyenas" that "contemporaneous crime is commonplace" to raise our hackles, but he is not quite willing to call Kaiser Wilhelm and the Empress of China criminal or to equate them with his historical criminals like Caracalla, Attila, Tamerlane, and Ivan. In fact, Wilhelm and the Empress become proof of the commonplaceness of contemporary crime. Saltus really prefers to use his present-day examples to get to his past examples which are so much more interesting and perhaps so much more acceptable. In "Human Hyenas" he weakens his fire further when he concludes with an attack on the contemporary press which makes his comments on crime and the subconscious merely trivial. "Power," he insists, "even when backed by bayonets, is powerless before the press."[14] He may be recalling his own treatment by the press at the time of his divorce. The drop from murder and the subconscious is sudden and disportionate.

What he had begun with, the fascination with the abnormal, the book of bad men that has yet to be written, he dissipates. His apologia for wickedness goes only so far. He acknowledges the fascination of the wicked, bravely calls them abnormal and wonders at the pleasure the "normal" derive from gawks at the abnormal, but he never makes good evil and evil good as the Marquis de Sade does.

During the later 1890's, when Saltus was writing for popular magazines, the two political events which excited his comment were the Spanish-American War and the exploitation of China by Western powers. He had more than once called war the chronic condition of history. He had even called it "murder glorified." He went on: "War is the paradox of jurisprudence. It sanctions that which it has forbidden, honors that which it punishes and rewards that which it reproves."[15] It substitutes the triumphal arch for the scaffold.

But his unsentimental view of war did not keep Saltus from supporting the Spanish-American War. A number of his pre-war columns detail the contributions of Spain to history: the world will owe her a notable debt "whether we eat her up or whether we don't."[16] His sense of Spain's former greatness and permanent contributions, or his sense of Cuba's history or Puerto Rico's beauty, did not relate to or conflict with his defense of empire. He could not resist analogy: a nation "resembles love: when it does not increase it diminishes." And the United States, presumably, ought to increase. Besides, Spanish colonial rule was tyrannous. Saltus snipes at Charles Eliot Norton for his attack on "the present war as inglorious," even accusing him of treason.[17] Such extravagant patriotism from so sophisticated a commentator, such a great desire for an imperial United States, tells us a great deal about the spirit of support for this war. But Saltus was outdone by Theodore Roosevelt, who remarked: "It wasn't much of a war, but it was the best war we had."

For the war that began in April and was over in August, Saltus had flippant as well as supportive comment. He also admired Pascual Cervera when Cervera's own government, considering defeat equivalent to poor soldiering, dishonored the admiral. Less than two weeks after the end of hostilities Saltus called the war "quite as decisive, almost as rapid, and certainly more comic than any other ever waged."[18] He had earlier suggested that the United States wanted an occasion for war, which it found in the explosion of the *Maine*. (The cause of that explosion is still uncertain.) That "there is glory in war, frequently frontiers and always coin" he knew and said. Elsewhere he altered his phrasing slightly, saying that the incentive for war is always coin or expansion "which is the same thing in the end." He also suggests that this ancient pattern may be undergoing a change, since business may find peace more profitable than war. He concludes: it is "safe to assume that war as a sport is declining. There is another game that pays better now"—business.[19]

The mixture of realism and imperialism makes Saltus' point of view a common one, perhaps a typical one. He is in elegant company. Brooks Adams also defended America's imperial urges and actions. Like Henry Adams, or other contemporary commentators, Saltus foresees a world convulsion whose combatants "will refurbish geography, tear out whole pages and set them up anew." The motion of rise, decline, and fall has seen Greece, Rome, Spain, and England play its turn on the stage of world empire: "The turn of Russia is coming. So is ours." "The war for the grab bag" was very much on in China, and although Anglo-Russian rivalry in China elicits Saltus' frequent comment, he also remembers the United States and suggests that she too pull a plum out of the grab bag. But his greed is under some control; in another article he suggests non-interference with Russia's activities because Russia has been "a civil neighbor and a good friend" and because "the plums in our own garden are big enough to compensate for any deficit in the grab bag out there."[20]

Apparently the Russification of the East was not to conflict with the law of nature which would presently "precipitate Canada upon us," as well as the Caribbean and the lands of the Incas and the Aztecs. Such dreams of a pole-to-pole empire were probably sober by comparison with wilder imperial dreams of the day. They were frank. And they are buttressed by a theory of inevitability: "We may not want them, and at present certainly we do not, but we cannot interfere with the law of gravitation." This is the pleasantest type of responsibility, the kind that is thrust upon us as we try to shy away from the honor. Within such a rationale, the possibility that those we are about to civilize do not want our civilization is inconceivable. The forces of history are inevitable and impersonal. The redistribution of the world between Russia and the United States will be "logical, evolutionary, and, though revolutionary, too, will, when accomplished, be accepted, as the inevitable always is."[21]

The basis for empire, therefore, lies in the forces of history and not in ideology. The sleeping East and a crumbled, irresponsible Spanish empire brought no horrified moral reactions from Saltus; Germany and the Kaiser did. Saltus joined the violently pro-war and anti-German majority during World War I; to him, the Germans were swine. He urged young men to join him, and he turned against the philosophy which had once inspired him: "the theories with which Germany is hallucinated" must go along with the Hohenzollerns. In a number of articles written for the New York *Herald*, only his criticism of the Empress Dowager of China is more severe than his criticism of Kaiser Wilhelm.

Saltus asserts war is the national industry of Prussia and finds it "ridiculous to have Berlinese soprani and bubonic bassi bleating here." He supports United States entry into the war, identifying the Huns as descendants of the barbarians who caused the fall of Rome, and who may again kill civilization.[22] The argument is familiar, particularly since most educated Americans had a powerful cultural and emotional commitment to France that easily generated anti-Germanism. Saltus wrote a pamphlet or pamphlets for the United States government. Edith Wharton worked hard for the Allied cause. A number of young writers like E. E. Cummings, Hemingway, John Dos Passos, and William Faulkner joined French, Canadian, or Italian units before their country entered the war. The cause was right, and very few contemporaries talked of coin or expansion. Edgar Saltus forgot coin and expansion to take a stand with the majority.

His comments on domestic politics are automatic and referential. His novels are sprinkled with market drops and panics which rarely affect his characters. "The *corridas* of the Street" he taunts, "don't differ much from those of Spain. In each case the spectacle is the same. It is the climax that varies. There the ring is swept by a supe, here it is struck by a crisis. The orbit of that crisis the astrogists of political economy figure at about ten years."[23] The comparison could not have pleased gentlemen active on the Stock Exchange.

Saltus usually shows no interest in issues related to the upper-class New Yorker in business. But the issue of crises, panics, depressions was national and chronic. Was there a solution? Saltus shows a surprising astuteness in his criticism of Andrew Carnegie's paternalistic solution to class inequities and economic crises: "The pseudo-benevolence of the idea is revolting. The masses don't want these things. They care nothing for parks that don't provide amusement, for art that doesn't appeal, for books that only bewilder, or for churches that no longer console. What they want is not soft solder, but socialism."[24]

As usual, Saltus will not allow so serious a statement to remain in his essays without adding the inevitable qualification that turns the insight into an aberration rather than a center. He immediately continues: "In default of the latter, then, if only for the pleasurable emotions that the circus provides, they want the spectacle of rich men living richly." So Saltus proposes the old bread-and-circuses, or just-circuses-if-there-is-no-bread theory of social stability, a solution as pseudo as Carnegie's that millionaires must relieve public needs. His proposal may represent a deliberate attempt to mock Carnegie's proposal with one more absurd, for the essay ends in deliberate absurdity as Saltus imagines our new millionaires in "Heliogabalan luxury, in super-Neronian magnificence, and in Vesuvii of coin," eventually giving automobiles and grand pianos away as cotillon favors.[25] Such hyperbole must be deliberate, the reader thinks. But is it? We can dream of gold even if we don't get it or have it, he goes on; therefore, the gospel of gold serves the poor as well as the rich. The unsureness of tone does not reside in his power or desire to astonish the bougeoisie; it resides in his own unsureness and evasion. He has dissipated his satiric gift.

He knew of Boss Croker's existence as he surely knew more about political and business corruption than the daily press told him, but he reserves his extended discussion for foreign affairs.[26] He may have done so by design, by assignment, or by the accident of having begun his journalistic writings when relations with Spain had displaced panics and strikes on page one. The kind of learning he had acquired could be better displayed with a foreign event, person, or nation as its take-off point. Even for feature articles like "Kings of the Highways and High Seas" his examples are all foreign: Jack the Slip String, Dick Turpin, Cartouche, Jonathan Wild, Captain Kidd, Walter Raleigh, Francis Drake, Henry Morgan.[27] His delight in such figures, in romantic highwaymen and pirates who can act outside the law, is a delight satisfied today by heroes of the American West. Saltus would probably have been one of the first to sense the popular value of the cowboy or of the outlaw. He had suggested in one of his *Collier's* editorial columns that only a "cinematograph" could fully satisfy the public thirst for the sight and feel of the Spanish-American War.

Official despatches, bulletins, press reports, special articles, no matter how good they are, "lack the actuality of the visible. Bulletins of battles are exceeded in dullness only by chronicles of crime."[28] Jules Michelet, the French historian, "the great somnambulist of history," gives the reader "the rumble of battle and the smoke of it, not the fight itself." Therefore, "Commodore Watson should take a cinematograph along" because "we want our money's worth" out of the war. The surface cynicism divulges a truth: Saltus as historian is Saltus as "cinematograph." He saw history with the movie-camera man's eye for vivid, brief glimpses of blood and drama, more frequently giving his reader long shots of masses and materials than close-ups. His search for his "money's worth" is a version of his search for the thrill in history, in crime, in politics.

His political views are conventional except for the sharp gleams which indicate an astuteness he preferred not to use consistently and thoroughly. In his support of empire and estheticism he suggests the joining of the two cultures represented by the *Yellow Book* and the Yellow Press. Holbrook Jackson, who beautifully brought together these two terms, sees not only the differences between the two yellows, which is easy, but the similarities between them, which was not so easy:

> The characteristic excitability and hunger for sensation are exemplified in the one as much as the other, for what after all was the "brilliance" of Vigo Street but the "sensationalism" of Fleet Street seen from the cultured side? Both were the outcome of a society which had absorbed a bigger idea of life than it knew how to put into practice, and it is not surprising to those who look back upon the period to find that both tendencies, in so far as they were divorced from the social revolution of the Nineties, were nihilistic, the one finding its Moscow at the Old Bailey, in 1895, the other in South Africa, in 1899.[29]

It is tempting to apply Jackson's symbolic formulation to the United States. The political analogue is good, for the Spanish-American War has been called "Hearst's war." The literary analogue is more imprecise even though it is true that 1895, the year of Oscar Wilde's trial, coincides with a distinct drop in the bohemian and decadent movement in the United States.[30] It is also true that Saltus' productivity noticeably slacks off in 1895 and that his journalistic career begins then. But the literary critic must soon stop, given the fragility of the esthetic movement in the United States and the imprecision of the analogical approach. Nevertheless, symbolically, the two "yellows" represent two forces that define and even engender each other. The Yellow Press won in both countries as the century came to an end amid jingoism and athleticism.

III *Beauty and Love*

If history showed to Saltus the crimes attendant on coin and expansion, she also showed the power of love. Tancred Ennever, the fictional hero of *When Dreams Come True* (1895), conceives of and begins a history of the heroines of love from Helen of Troy to the present. Tancred, who finds his love, is more fortunate than most Saltus heroes who assume that love is the key to happiness and discover that it is not or that it is overrated. Saltus earlier, his heroes later, proclaim intensely that love, happiness, and beauty are illusions; and they do so with the fury that only those who once believed, or still believe, can have. Neither Saltus nor his heroes ever quite recovered from the discrepancy between expectation and fulfillment.

Saltus, like Tancred Ennever, may himself already have been at work on a three-volume compendium for P. F. Collier called *The Lovers of the World* (1896-7). The work, a "scissors and paste" job, as Saltus called his Collier's histories, represents the cursory sacking of sources for coin.[31] From Helen of Troy, Penelope and Ulysses, Dido and Aeneas down through the centuries to his last example, Victoria and Albert (exalted surely by the company), Saltus parades the lovers of myth and history. Almost everyone is there: Lohengrin, Faust, Heloise, Petrarch, Nell Gwynne, Stella, Vanessa, Don Juan, their partners, and many others. What Saltus "got up," as he put it, about historical lovers he was to use again and again in other books and essays. Yet beyond the surface manipulation of saleable data lies a fascination or, more accurately, an obsession with love and ladies.

The fascination shows in novels and essays that antedate his Collier's potboiler. Saltus uses, for example, two essays in *Love and Lore* (1890) which examine the medieval courts of love and their canons of courtesy to spoof contemporary courting and social codes. The cases and decisions of the older courts might, if adopted today, inject some life into a social atmosphere that "has in it the opacity and heaviness of a room long closed . . . it is infected with ennui." Such courts and the use of King Arthur's codes instead of Blackstone's may bring to Fifth Avenue "one day at least of sheer and perfect joy."[32]

The essays, far more than the novels, contain the quotable lines that his contemporaries remembered him for. Their style is staccato and epigrammatic; their content almost frivolous. A later attempt to define love begins with the conflict between love and art, leaves it, and continues as a compendium of all the paradoxes of love which concludes with the sophisticated surface cynicism of the final definition:

> . . . apart from pathological conditions, love is either the affection of somebody else or else the fusion of two egotisms, the contact of two epiderms, the tragedy of those that lack it, the boredom of those that don't, and in this country the prime incentive to matrimony, which also studies and statistics have led us to regard as three months of adoration, three months of introspection, and thirty years of toleration, with children to begin it all over anew. *Et voilà ce que c'est que l'Amour.*[33]

In the same mood, we may respond to a typical inversion: "it is better to have loved your wife than never to have loved at all." Perhaps, Saltus suggests with similar frivolity, we ought to have Chairs of Love and Lucre in our universities. If these two items are the motor forces of society, then our academies ought to teach us how to get them.

The American heiress, the country's most exportable commodity, may represent the happiest conjunction of these two forces. Unfortunately, "every one of them loves a lord, though it is not every one of them who has a lord to marry." Saltus asks us to help these lovely, capable girls to attain their goal by making titles purchasable in America. The young lady who gets her titled husband soon so changes that "no one dreams that she once had a twang, that she lived in a land of savages and dressed in feathers and beads." When the lord turns to other women, the little girl "will sit and weep, and if she is a good little girl, as all nice little American girls are supposed to be, she will sit and weep alone."[34]

Irony, extravagance, and a touch of absurdity define the Saltus posture toward the inhabitants of Vanity Square. Nevertheless, in this essay on the heiress, "Vanity Square," and in two others, "Our Foreign Princesses" and "The Heiress," Saltus exhibits a fondness for the young girl and a concern for the special dangers her money creates.

He is not so genial toward the Gilded Gang from which the American heiress derives. He complains that members of her class who make up what he called in a comically happy moment of rhetorical exaggeration, "the mammoth menageries of money-getters," no longer "sin and sparkle."[35] Why the American provincials come "from the pampas, the savannahs, the mines" to join them, he cannot imagine; for, "never, perhaps, except in the Rome of the Caesars, has there been gathered together in one city a set so rich, so idle, so profoundly uninterested in anything save themselves. No wonder there are proletarians."[36] The final non-sequitur may stand for Saltus at his best subversive self.

It is not surprising to find that near the turn of the century Saltus' voice begins to take on a strident tone as he laments the world being created by the new industrial society. To hear the "shriek of steam where gods have strayed" signals the death of beauty. The lament for the passing of beauty elicits a judgment classic to the Decadent point of view: "where utility and ugliness reign the useless and the beautiful retreat." So the world becomes "uglier and more comfortable day by day."[37] The sorcery of beauty, like that of the rose, is to charm and do nothing. The view that the function of beauty is to be and not to do is ancient; its Greek roots are reflected in the Bible's "consider the lilies of the field; they toil not, neither do they spin." To insist on such gospel against the contrary one of work—which had become the gospel of gold—was eccentric, irresponsible, probably immoral and may still be.[38] If the doctrine, as Saltus expresses it, appears inadequate, it is not because we have learned that beauty and utility are not necessarily enemies, but because Saltus used it to retreat rather than to engage. Despite its simplicity, it represents an important countercurrent to the gospel of work and gold which a society contemplating even more hours of leisure will need to re-examine.[39]

Saltus' vision of the future contains only "trusts and machinery." Trusts, machinery, and comfort—the vision is related to Aldous Huxley's *Brave New World*, not to George Orwell's *1984*. As such, the Saltus future is a projection of later nineteenth-century experience rather than a projection of the wars and politics of the twentieth century. For Saltus, progress is a comfortable disease. But his training in history, no matter how superficial experts may declare it to have been, did not allow him to rest entirely in nostalgia for a more satisfactory past. One of his major axioms militated against his posture as exhausted bystander: "Nothing is constant but change. Life alone resists the mutation of things."[40] So in his essays he frequently and anti-climactically allows for a return of the beauty and the love he sees disappearing.

His own New York City bore fit witness to deterioration: "Once the Cinderella of cities," New York has become "the noisiest, greediest, least habitable of cities." The continual displacement of the heart of Manhattan, usually in an uptown direction, will end in the heart's complete displacement until New York will be entirely a "market instead of a city." In his own time Saltus had seen Fifth Avenue turn commercial. He could already say of his New York that, "Except in the Plaza region, it is residentially defunct." If his apt term admits of qualification, then New York is even more "residentially defunct" than it was. Still one of the "least habitable" and most inhabited of cities, still tending to become a city of "mice and millionaires," New York could then and now illustrate Dante's Inferno:

> From the Battery to Harlem, then, Manhattan will be one vast bazaar, wholly commercial, utterly heartless, thronged day by day, vacant by night, a sort of glowing Gehenna, into which each morning from Long Island, from Jersey, from Connecticut, from regions remoter yet, hordes of human beings will pour and plot and scheme for gold, toil and trick for it, contrive and fight, and, when the horrible day is done, scurry back to their warrens, to their soap-bubble loves and hates.[41]

The essentials of the prediction are still in progress. His "glowing Gehenna" is not the city seen from the point of view of the provincial young man or woman. It is the city become Megalopolis. This essay, "The Heart of Manhattan," ends not with the postulate that beauty will return again as it always has, but with an injunction to his readers to examine Doré's drawings for *The Inferno.* Traditional patrician lament for a society "smeared with trade" defines only part of Saltus' attitude, for he could be both cutting and comfortable. In his rage against the destruction of the community he knew he was entirely cutting.

Perhaps trusts and machinery had played their share in the erosion of the talent of Edgar Saltus. When he turned to his next non-fiction work on love, he had had ten years to mull over the material that had gone into his potboiler for Collier's. In *Historia Amoris: A History of Love Ancient and Modern* (1906), he surveys concepts and practitioners of love as he was to survey the gods and goddesses of religion the next year in *Lords of the Ghostland* (1907). *Historia Amoris* is better than *Lovers of the World,* which becomes almost anonymous by its lack of a style and a point of view. In *Historia Amoris,* Saltus applies his later style to a conception of love as a goddess who multiplied and multiplies herself endlessly from Ishtar of Babylonia to Astarte, Tanit, Ashtoroth, and other incarnations of the goddess.

Saltus is interested in getting at the nature of love through her appearances in earlier civilizations like the Babylonian, the Hebraic, the Greek, the Roman, and the medieval. Although he is still compiling examples of love, his decision to conclude with the Marquis de Sade is brave and intelligent. Aware of the rare irony that the Marquis is a "lineal descendant of Petrarch's Laura," Saltus uses his knowledge to underline his view of the development of love. The Marquis "set the infernal in the divine" to become the fit symbol and "logical climax to which decadence had groped and to it already the austere guillotine was attending."[42] Although the work may be nearly vitiated by its surface, summaristic approach, its use of de Sade is original as is, for example, its discussion of Moorish influence, particularly through the Cordova caliphate whose poets precede the troubadours.

If the book has a thesis, it is that love, like beauty, is exempt from the law of change ("change is the one thing constant") since its essence remains through all its changes of dress. The final pages remain a paean to the evolutionary development of love from "the shames of Ishtar" to a future we cannot yet see but which may well make today's man seem an ape to his descendant. If man comes closer to god, love will have effected his advance: "it has changed the face of the earth. It has transformed laws and religions. It has reversed and reconstructed every institution human and divine."[43]

In a privately printed essay, *The Gardens of Aphrodite* (1920), Saltus presents the male incarnation of Eros—Don Juan. Like Eros, his embodiments are multiple and mythical: "He fathered the Wandering Jew. He assisted at the birth of Faust. He antedates Mammon. Protean, indefinite, eternal, he is the oldest and the youngest being on earth. Born in the Garden of Karma, his avatars are as many as Vishnu's, his masks as multiple as his amours."[44]

Saltus bows to the power of Eros and maintains that "at heart every man is a Don Juan." Shame, spite, and jealousy have no place beside the true Aphrodite; nor does chastity, so frequently "a recognized aberration" in ancient times. The point of view that man is not monogamous has lengthy and ancient testimonials; and Saltus, as expected, invokes history. Although he bows to the demiurgic power of love, he insists, as always, that it cannot bring happiness, that fulfillment is equivalent to disenchantment, that there is no tale of love without melancholy or tragedy at its heart. Love's characteristic refrain is: "Sono l'Amore, difida di me." In effect, he describes love as an elemental force of nature, amoral, turbulent, eternal. What man and morality can do before the demiurge of love is simple—helplessly and delightedly submit to it.

Love, despite disenchantment and the "infernal feminine," functions for Saltus as mythos, as a god in a time when traditional religious belief had been considerably eroded. "The hour in the history of life when there were altars to love," when she had divinity, had gone. Saltus might suggest that contemporary "pilgrims of passion" could find "another Mecca" in the pavilion in the forest of Mayerling where Prince Rudolph and Mary died; but such a suggestion, as he must have known, sentimentalized the goddess.[45] His magazine copy on royal romances, champion prisoners and poisoners, fashions, food, perfumes, and paradises serves quite overtly as escape mechanisms. But Saltus treated these essays as lightly as a severe critic might. He called one collection, *The Pomps of Satan,* after "those pomps of Satan which the provincial press currently and collectively describes as etiquette."[46] He justly, then, placed his magazine writings by which too many critics have judged the whole Saltus.

He may still be vulnerable to the charge of escapism. In Schopenhauer's suggestion that art is one means of alleviating the affliction of life, Saltus may have found a complement to certain tenets of estheticism. The paradox is that even escape must be managed with the total conviction that Saltus could not quite muster. He could, however, project the unexpected possibilities of escape in light discussions of poisons, drugs, paradises and other possible pleasures. His postures and positions were to become more common during the 1920's; indeed, hindsight, or literary history, may prefer to say he anticipated that decade. He understands the case for excess although he was only in a very limited way to become an example of it.

History, he had said, "is illuminated with crimes that have been applauded and absolved because of their inherent beauty."[47] He had connected crime and beauty; in strife and love he had seen, like some of the early Greek philosophers, the dialectic that defines life, that creates act and change. Above that dialectic he had placed beauty as the unifying agent of the universe. Even in love, he had looked below pleasant surfaces and been fascinated by the work of Richard von Krafft-Ebing ("a scientist of real value"), Jean Charcot, Pierre Janet, Havelock Ellis.[48] At his most exaggerated, Saltus seems a Sir Epicure Mammon, a comic would-be voluptuary in his fantasies of love and material delights. Like his esthetic contemporaries in England and France, a Wilde or a Huysmans, he suggests a libertinism he never actually practiced in his art or in his life. The suggestions were apparently enough for his audience—an unfortunate situation since a more astringent opposition, one more intelligent and involved, might have wrested a deeper response out of the writers of the 1880's and 1890's.

To have sensed the connection between obsessional love and crime required acumen in a layman of the later nineteenth century. Saltus did not develop the connection—less because he was a layman than because he characteristically did not develop and deepen his often acute insights. That he broached a new way of seeing the connection between love and war in terms of abnormal psychology and economic determinism is to his credit. That he functioned so frequently, therefore, as historian and amorist is not surprising since what was polar did interconnect. What more exquisite occupation than to examine and adjust the relationships between the shudders of pain and of pleasure, of Ares and Eros? That adjustment could focus on Rome, Russia, and contemporary wars as easily as upon historical lovers, *don juanisme*, and local examples of ideal and aberrational love. The focus was that of the cinematographer—sharp, fleeting, popular. Nevertheless it was there—right on what continues to absorb so many students of human behavior.

Afterword

What it comes back to, in other words, is the intensity with which we live—and his intensity is recorded for us on every page of his work.

HENRY JAMES, "The Lesson of Balzac"

LIKE HENRY JAMES and other American contemporaries, Edgar Saltus had searched in his paradoxist way for "the human note in the huge American rattle of gold."[1] His point of view and his career support the thesis of many writers of the 1920's that post-Civil War America was inhospitable if not hostile to the artist. The nation's inhospitality did not mean Saltus could not find publishers, for the poison was subtler and more pervasive. It had to do with a point in time and a way of life which engendered, as Matthew Josephson believed, "the exotic, aborted, or estranged careers of American artists."[2] Josephson modified only a little the Van Wyck Brooks thesis that the American environment corrupts or corrodes artistic ability.

But Edgar Saltus is not in any obvious sense a victim of that environment. One critic commented, "Mr. Saltus came on the stage a little too late and very much too soon."[3] He may be right, for Saltus would more easily have found his place as a writer in pre-Civil War and post-World War I America. Within his own period, only the very best could produce at the high level of excellence that Saltus could recognize if not emulate.

Saltus was, with contemporaries like James Huneker, Vance Thompson, and Percival Pollard, at the very least, "a Service."[4] In his role as a cultural middleman, he brought to the newer and growing middle-class audience news of French and other European literatures and habits.[5] He helped to make American literary insularity impossible. The 1920's completed his job. He and his "decade of small things" anticipated other concerns and interests of the 1920's. His criticism of the American cultural environment included, for example, explicit use of the

Puritan past as scapegoat and explicit awareness of the simplicities of the art-morality debates of the period. The Saltus who coined "Bourgeoisophobus" suggests some relationship with the Mencken who coined "booboisie." Both writers flourished when genius was more often equated with immorality than it is today. The existence of an avant-garde (now that it is dead, it is taken for granted) had its beginnings as an idea and as a fact in the American climate of opinion that included Saltus. This avant-garde insisted on craftsmanship and risked being called "esthetic" for that insistence.[6] The bare, early Saltus style, departing radically from classic nineteenth-century American prose style, is closer to twentieth-century practice. Saltus also looked eagerly to discoveries in psychology; he was particularly fascinated with pathology. Pathology might describe, if not explain, what happened to his deluded lovers. He saw the dust beneath the gilt and accepted in pessimism a thin explanation for frustration and reality. But pessimism allowed him to become an early subverter of "uplift."

His novels are transparent footnotes to pessimistic doctrine in which he tries to remind his confident contemporaries that "Happiness is a myth invented by Satan for our despair."[7] Although the novels are more ornamental than profoundly disenchanting, they are based on the discordance between idea and existence which erupts in disillusion and violence—a subject central to human experience that has had its special relevance in American literature. Saltus' interest in economics and politics, in the ecology of empire, and in the decay of the city was not accidental. He saw with Henry James that "nowhere else does pecuniary power so beat its wings in the void" as in the United States.[8] But he lacked major talent, adequate allies, and the audience (it could be small; it had to be supportive) to make his nibbling at materialism and provincialism sufficiently telling.

His was not merely a general disaffection for life; he was convinced of the special destructiveness of modern life. His ennui was not peculiar. It joins a long tradition of laments characteristic of the Romantic temperament for the loss of enthusiasm, of joy, of creative power. In his search for a credo, Saltus also joins other artists. He chose pessimism, theosophy, or elements of estheticism to supplant voids left by the failures of the dominant nineteenth-century systems of political and religious thought.

His pessimism was more like stoicism or epicureanism than cynicism. He did not agree with Max Nordau, a preacher of dire decline before Spengler, that genius is morbid. For Saltus, not genius but pseudo-genius is morbid.[9]

Saltus managed to get his relatively sophisticated knowledge into the most unlikely places. In a New York *Journal* article on "An American Heiress's Melancholy Downfall," his introductory material is about Robert de Montesquiou, the original of Huysmans' Des Esseintes. Aware that de Montesquiou had, since his literary incarnation, been trying to live up to his fictional self, Saltus neatly and economically anatomizes the gentleman: "He was naif, yet depraved, with a pretty taste for paradox and a pertinacious desire to astound."[10] The severest Saltus critic might say the sentence anatomizes Saltus himself. He was, in a way, naif; for a man may have a knowledge of esoterica and still be naif. But he was not, as most 1890's figures were not, "depraved." And he knew and agreed with Aristotle that, although "art should always have a continual slight novelty . . . , a thing which startles or amazes is not art."[11]

When Saltus forgot, or could not follow, what he knew by virtue of his limited endowments, his own work lapsed. The fine art of shocking was an art worth cultivating in his time. When that art became for the later Saltus a desperate effort to rescue himself from the commonplace, it was no longer fine but fake. Thrill overthrew truth; the shudder became melodrama. Perhaps by then what had happened to one of his characters had happened to him: he had gotten used to monsters and could not exorcise them—"In certain conditions the soul gets used to monsters. It makes itself at home with what it must."[12] At such a stage, it is impossible to turn the rage of disenchantment into enduring prose. That he reached this stage is only partly due to the pressures of his time and place.

Although Saltus is more the eclectic than the eccentric he has generally been made out to be, he cannot be rescued from complicity in the corruptions that he had the courage to see but not to resist. He had a real gift for popular entertainment and comic exaggeration, but left no enduring single work which shows the combination and maturation of these gifts. In fact, his reputation rests rather lopsidedly on his "purples," his diabolisms, and his clever style. It ought to rest a little more evenly:

on several novels and on a number of his essays on society, manners, and trivia. Indeed, were the essay as popular as it once was, more readers would be enjoying Saltus. There is a residue of vision and conviction in Saltus left, even when posterity has completed her ruthless excisions from his work. More than the first-order writer, he reveals direct reactions to specific literary, cultural, and political issues of his era. For the social and intellectual historian, Saltus is, therefore, a prolific, highly coruscated and frequently sensitive register of the period.

Saltus might acknowledge the appropriateness of almost every epithet that has so far been ascribed to his era; it was "Mauve," "Brown," "Gilded," and "Innocent," but not "Confident" for him and for a number of his contemporaries. As a son of New York—from a family line that includes Van Dams, Hasbroucks, Howes, Reuters, and Roosevelts—and of a family history that sometimes analogues class, local, and national history in its movement from sea captains to merchants to iron ore producers to leisured dilettantes, he may tempt us to see in his career the death or attenuation of the Eastern Dutch-English literary ruling class. Saltus may finally represent the gifted aristocratic amateur now nearly extinct.

The American 1890's nourished no genius as the English 1890's nourished Yeats. This failure explains the essential discontinuity between the 1890's and the 1920's, between two generations that ought to have collaborated. Instead, the 1920's began again, with very little awareness than an earlier generation had begun its major battles. Within that earlier generation Saltus remains a first soldier. He was a frequently severe, brave, and witty critic of his own class and his own limitations. As his "mammoth menageries of money-getting" reminds us, he could have mastered the rhetoric of comic exaggeration. But at crucial points his courage falters and he dissipates his comic gift to become only sporadically subversive in an era that required fiercer and deeper subversion.

His self-proffered conflict is suggestive; it speaks for so much in the Romantic and in the specifically American Romantic temperament: "I was born with a lot of vices that never put their nose to the window. I like wine and never drink—I would gamble perhaps but I don't know one card from another—I am a mystic at heart and believe in nothing. Debauchery attracts me and I live like a monk."[13] His remarks make a specialized addition to the literature of America's fear and fascination for experience. The self-portrait is very likely a literary creation, but even its imagined accuracy or its very conception show that longing and frustration which made the man and the era "almost" decadent. If achievement does come back, as Henry James felt, to "the intensity with which we live," then Saltus' intensity is recorded for us only fitfully and during the brief span of some ten years. His pilgrimage was not sufficiently passionate. It could not, like his grandfather's, make "a wilderness a paradise"; but it could and did make a small and interesting garden.

Notes and References

I have used two abbreviations, VVC and ESC, to represent respectively the Carl Van Vechten and the Edgar Saltus Collections at Yale University.

Chapter One

1. Elbert Hubbard, "Heart to Heart Talks with Philistines by the Pastor of His Flock," *Philistine,* XXV (October, 1907), 139; Benjamin de Casseres, *Forty Immortals* (New York, 1926), pp. 89-90.

2. So Arthur Symons quotes Wilde in "A Note on Edgar Saltus," *Vanity Fair,* XIV (March, 1920), 71. Carl Van Vechten quotes a letter from James Huneker in "Edgar Saltus: A Postscript," *Double Dealer, II* (October, 1921), 162-63: "George Moore once told me that Walt Whitman and Saltus were the only two Americans he read." "We sit agape," Moore continues, "when we think of him [Saltus]," and wonder why, with his "brain and style," Saltus "did not achieve a really memorable piece of work."

Saltus' popularity among the forming avant-garde is suggested by his inclusion as a character in Huneker's *Painted Veils* (1920); reference to him in Carl Van Vechten's *Peter Whiffle* (1922); and, less expectedly, in Sinclair Lewis' *Ann Vickers* (1933); and in Hart Crane's letters. The Lewis heroine "could never abide Eula's real idols, Swinburne and Edgar Saltus and Oscar Wilde." Ann graduated college in 1912. Crane may have come to Saltus, whom he enjoyed, through Gorham Munson and Samuel Loveman. Elsie Saltus has in her possession an unpublished manuscript on Saltus by Samuel Loveman. Between 1919 and 1924 Crane refers to Saltus briefly in three letters to Munson and in one to his mother. See *The Letters of Hart Crane, 1916-1932,* ed. Brom Weber (New York, 1952).

3. Sadakichi Hartmann "The Edgar Saltus I Knew," *Bookman,* LXVIII (September, 1923), 17-19. The personal effects Saltus left at his death were unusually modest rather than opulent; they were valued at $100. Surrogate's Court, County of New York, Transfer Tax Records, P1583/1921.

4. Gorham Munson, "The Limbo of American Literature," *Broom,* II (June, 1922), 257. The suggestion is unlikely. See H. L. Mencken's "Hiring A Hall," New York *World,* October 11, 1925. In this article, later reprinted in *Prejudices: Fifth Series* (New York, 1926), Mencken

also erroneously lists *The Truth About Tristrem Varick* as the first Saltus novel.

5. Harry Hansen, "Unveiling Edgar Saltus," Chicago *Daily News*, September 30, 1925.

6. Letter, Saltus to Carl Van Vechten, January 18, 1918. VVC, Yale.

7. *Who's Who* and most other sources list 1858 as the Saltus birthdate. Edgar wrote in a letter to the Editors of the Library of American Literature that he was "born in this city on the 8th of October 1858." See letter to E. C. Stedman, October 28, 1889, Columbia University. The Municipal Archives have no record of Edgar's birth; but according to the records of the Collegiate Dutch Reformed Church in New York City, Edgar was born October 5, 1855 and baptized June 24, 1856.

8. Mencken, "Hiring A Hall." Keith Preston, wittily accusing Marie Saltus of theosophizing rather than psychoanalyzing her husband, found Karmas a "refreshing change from complexes." See "The Periscope," Chicago *News*, October 6, 1925. Mrs. Saltus was herself the author of *The End of the Journey, Her Game of Consequences, Though Her Sins Be As Scarlet,* and other works.

9. Quoted in Ethel Saltus Ludington, *The Ludington-Saltus records*, ed. Louis Effingham de Forest (New Haven, 1925), pp. 52-53. Saltus' birthdate is here inaccurate. The article on the Saltus family in *Colonial Families of America*, XIII (New York, 1933), pp. 335-49, is more accurate.

10. Francis and Francis Henry owned an iron ore mine or mines in Clintonville, New York, which Francis Henry sold to a group chartered in April 1865 as Peru Iron and Steel Company with an $800,000 capital. It has so far been difficult to discover more than this except that "several fortunes" were realized from the mine concerned. See C. Winslow Watson, *The Military and Civil History of the County of Essex, New York* (Albany, 1869), p. 449. It seems likely that Francis Henry sold the family business about this time. The last New York City Directory entry for Saltus & Company and for Francis Henry himself is in the 1867-1868 volume.

11. Ludington, *Ludington-Saltus Records,* p. 54.

12. Marie Saltus, *Edgar Saltus: The Man* (New York, 1925), p. 10.

13. Whoever went to school was likely to attend a private academy. There were only one hundred public schools in the entire country at the outbreak of the Civil War. The records of St. Paul's show that Saltus was a student of the class of 1872 and attended for only one year, from September, 1871, to June, 1872. There is no record of his education before that time. No grades for the period exist, but

Saltus is not listed as one of the exceptionally good students. His studies for his year of attendance probably included the traditional fifth-form subjects: Sacred Studies, Latin, Greek, English, mathematics and natural philosophy. Information based on a letter from the Rector's Secretary at St. Paul's to the author, August 19, 1964. The school is Episcopal.

In connection with her dissertation, "Literary Techniques, Backgrounds, and Ideas of Edgar Saltus" (University of Wisconsin, 1953, p. 24), Ruth Elizabeth Stephenson received a letter from Henry M. Fuller, Reference Librarian of the Yale University Library, dated June 19, 1952, describing the two semesters Saltus completed in geometry, Latin, Greek and algebra. There is no record of grades for fall 1872. For the fall of 1873, "he had two passes and two failures. . . . We have no record of him in the second term, January to Easter, or the third term, Easter to June, and we have no record of his taking the annual examinations."

Edgar Saltus had considerable formal education for the period. One of the striking developments of the period was the Harvard elective system; another was the beginning of graduate training. Although the first American Ph.D. was conferred by Yale in 1861, the Yale Graduate School was not organized till 1871. Graduate training was, therefore, infrequent and usually acquired abroad. As Saltus' own training shows, a college degree was not then a prerequisite to a law degree.

14. Marie Saltus, *Edgar Saltus: The Man*, p. 21. Mrs. Saltus suggests Edgar had a "slight hesitancy" of speech. Charles Hanson Towne, a *Smart Set* editor who knew Edgar, says, in "A Number of Things," "He had a slight impediment in his speech which added to his charm rather than detracted from it." From an unidentified column in a New York Hearst newspaper, c. 1921, in Elsie Welsh Saltus' private collection. Reprinted with minor alterations in Charles Hanson Towne, *Adventures in Editing* (New York, 1926), pp. 82-84.

15. Compare Lenox Leigh, Saltus' first doomed patrician intellectual, who has vague literary aspirations and says, with a Wildean self-thrust: "If I have not written heretofore, it is because it seems more original not to do so" (*Mr. Incoul's Misadventure*, p. 199). Ralph Marvell, the hero of Edith Wharton's *The Custom of the Country,* who keeps his unfinished sketches and poetry in a cupboard, comes from a similar tradition: "Nothing in the Dagonet and Marvell tradition was opposed to this desultory dabbling with life. For four or five generations it had been the rule of both houses that a young fellow should go to Columbia or Harvard, read law, and then lapse into more or less cultivated inaction." Unexpectedly enough, Saltus is listed in the New York City Directory for two years (1882-1884)

as a lawyer and for one of those two years (1882-1883) he has a business address (152 Broadway).

16. James Huneker, *Steeplejack* (New York, 1923), 11, pp. 12-13.

17. H. L. Mencken describes the after-effects of a conversation with Huneker: "It was, in brief, chaos, and chaos cannot be described. But it was chaos made to gleam and coruscate with every device of the seven arts—chaos drenched in all the colors imaginable, chaos scored for an orchestra which made the great band of Berlioz seem like a fife and drum corps." *Prejudices* (New York, 1922), 66-68.

18. The Brander Matthews Collection at Columbia University contains five letters from Francis Saltus to Brander Matthews.

19. Huneker, *Steeplejack*, II, 13.

20. Marie Saltus, *Edgar Saltus: The Man*, p. 11.

21. Perhaps Marie saw Edgar as a member of the group that played with Stanford White. The aura of that play is recaptured in Huneker's *Painted Veils* (New York, 1920) in which the pie-girl dinner given by Henry Poor is memorialized, with trimmings. The *News Letter* of San Francisco for February 23, 1907, wondered if Harry Thaw's murder of Stanford White on June 25, 1906, inspired *The Perfume of Eros* (1905) or was inspired by the novel. In a letter dated March 8, 1907, Saltus replied that his novel was already in print when White was killed and was not in any case meant to incite imitative action.

22. Elsie Welsh Saltus has in her possession a copy of a wedding certificate which contradicts the formerly accepted second marriage in Paris in 1895. The copy, dated June 28, 1910, shows that Elsie Smith and Edgar were married in London on December 17, 1894. Edgar listed his age as thirty-seven; Elsie listed her as as twenty-nine. General Register Office, Somerset House, London, #11702.

23. New York *Herald*, Sunday, June 21, 1891, nonuple sheet.

24. It is generally agreed that scandal attendant on the divorce of Percival Pollard in 1899 caused his retirement to Connecticut. He was fortunate in one sense: he wrote his best work from his Connecticut retreat.

25. Marie Saltus, *Edgar Saltus:* The Man, pp. 56, 61.

26. See the letter of F. H. Saltus to E. C. Stedman from Greenwich, Conn., April 2, 1891. See also three letters to John M. Ross, June 4, June 9, 1894, and May 11, 1904, in which Francis Henry expresses his pleasure in being able to answer questions about his son to an admirer. E. C. Stedman Collection, Columbia University.

27. *Time*, p. 3. Undated scrapbook clipping. ESC, Yale.

28. "Ghosts," in *Uplands of Dream*, ed. Charles Honce (Chicago, 1925), p. 30. Fawcett inscribed the novel, *A Demoralizing Marriage*

(1889): "To My Friend Edgar Saltus In Recognition of His Distinct Genius, in Affectionate Appreciation of His Rapid Success as a Novelist, and in the Hope that Many Years May Pass Before All His Brilliant Gifts of Story-Telling Shall Cease to Charm their Loyal Listeners." Saltus inscribed his *Love and Lore* (1890): "To Edgar Fawcett, Perfect Poet—Perfect Friend." A different kind of response appears in Notebook Two; it reads: "Idleness is necessary to the artist . . . Be idle Mrs. Fawcett, let others toil, be idle and give us a rest." ESC, Yale.

29. Did Saltus need money? Geoffrey T. Hellman in "Can the Rich Write" in the *New Yorker* of June 8, 1963, p. 46, notices the discrepancy between Van Wyck Brooks's assumption in the *Confident Years: 1885-1915* (New York, 1952), p. 114, that Saltus was, like his hero Tancred Ennever, " 'born with a gold spoon in his mouth'," and Marie Saltus' remark that Edgar had only "a small inheritance from his father" and "what little Mr. Saltus had was in stocks and bonds."

When Francis Henry died in 1905, he left everything to his only surviving son, Edgar. No transfer tax record of his estate exists, which probably means one of two things: that there were insufficient assets or that Francis Henry turned whatever real or personal property he had over to his beneficiary before he died. In either case, no tax would be assessed and no record left of the senior Saltus' assets at the time of his death.

Edgar left nearly $60,000 when he died, most of it in very conservative gold bonds. Although that sum would be worth about four times its amount today, it is small by comparison with the almost $1,500,000 his first wife, Helen Read Oothout, left when she died in 1925. See Transfer Tax Records, Surrogate's Court, County of New York; for Saltus estate, P1583/1921; for Oothout estate, Nov. 18, 1926, P547/1925. Edgar's will also reveals that he left $16,000 to a woman other than his wife. (Marie received the remainder.) Arrangements for the bequest were made in 1919. Other evidence makes it clear that Marie knew of the relationship and was a friend of the woman.

30. New York *Tribune*, February 15, 1902, p. 6, col. 2.

31. Marie Saltus, *Edgar Saltus: The Man*, p. 82.

32. Letter, Saltus to Van Vechten, February 21, 1918. VVC, Yale.

33. *The Record of the Class of 1876, Yale College, 1876-1892* (New York, 1893), pp. 177-78. In an 1887 letter to the secretary of the Class of '77, Saltus claimed to "have received a degree of Ph.D. which I do not deserve, and a decoration which I do not wear." See *Yale Seventy-Seven: Their Lives and Letters Collected and Arranged for Private Distribution by the Secretary of the Class* (c. 1892), p. 291. No Ph.D. has turned up; the decoration is probably the one

which included the hereditary title of Marquis di Casa Bisa given to his father by the Portuguese government.

34. Letter, Saltus to Van Vechten, February 14, 1918. VVC, Yale.

35. Letter, Saltus to Van Vechten, February 25, 1919. VVC, Yale.

36. Letter, Saltus to Edward Bok. Saltus did not believe in happiness and would not give his youthful questioner a recipe for it. VVC, Yale.

37. The final quotations of the chapter are from Notebook Two. ESC, Yale.

Chapter Two

1. Saltus creates this twist of the Cartesian formula and applies it to Leopardi in *The Philosophy of Disenchantment* (New York, 1885), p. 19.

2. *Ibid.*, p. 220.

3. John Oxenford, "Iconoclasm in German Philosophy," *Westminster Review,* LIX (April, 1853), 388-407. Saltus refers to this article in his own review of the reception of Schopenhauer's ideas in *The Philosophy of Disenchantment,* p. 66.

4. The first signs of serious European recognition of Nietzsche (1844-1900) occur in 1888 through Hippolyte Taine and Georg Brandes. Holbrook Jackson in the *Eighteen-Nineties* dates the general interest in Nietzsche in England from 1896. The first translation of Nietzsche appeared in 1888. Mencken's public admiration of Nietzsche begins in 1908 in his *Philosophy of Frederick Nietzsche.* The chief early influences on Nietzsche were Wagner and Schopenhauer.

Accordng to Havelock Ellis in the *Encyclopedia of Religion and Ethics* ("Nietzsche," IX, 366-70), Nietzsche probably liked Schopenhauer's "constant appeal to the concrete and practical problems of living, . . . the beauty of his style" and his emphasis on specific values rather than on the architectonic coherence of previous German philosophic systems. Neither Schopenhauer nor Nietzsche is noted for his logical system; neither inspired schools. Both have had an unusually diffuse influence. Both are moralists, prophets, artists rather than philosophers in the strict sense.

These qualities explain Schopenhauer's appeal to Saltus and Nietzsche's appeal to Mencken. Saltus, by the way, indicates an early enjoyment of Wagner, an "incontestable genius," unlike Schopenhauer who, "it is said, shook his head at Wagner, and would have none of him; yet if Schopenhauer was ever wrong, he was certainly wrong in that." (*Philosophy,* p. 196). Music appears to be far more central to this earlier group than to the 1920's group. Huneker and Van Vechten were also closely allied to music. When Saltus characters go out of an evening, they go to the opera, not to the theater. Huneker makes a leading lady in his *Painted Veils* an opera diva, not an actress.

5. *Philosophy,* p. 35.

6. Compare Huneker on von Hartmann. He remarks on the "so-called new school of Freudian psychoanalysis, which exploits to the *reductio ad absurdum* the von Hartmann theory of the subliminal consciousness, with a little spice of sooth-saying and dream-book twaddle thrown in to lend an air of novelty. We learn from Dr. Freud that dreams are the result of unfulfilled desire . . . that authors unconsciously reveal themselves in their writings. What an astounding discovery! . . . Cut out the erotic element in this 'new' theory and the world would pass it by." New York *World,* November 16, 1919, Metropolitan Section, p. 6.

7. *Philosophy,* p. 166.

8. *Ibid.,* p. 187.

9. *Ibid.,* p. 149.

10. *Ibid.,* p. 223.

11. *Ibid.,* pp. 215, 217.

12. *Ibid.,* pp. 224, 234.

13. Robert Ingersoll wrote a nearly twenty-page prologue to Edgar Fawcett's *Agnosticism and Other Essays* (New York, 1889). The volume contains an essay entitled "The Arrogance of Optimism" which refers to superficial criticisms of Edgar Saltus' works.

Huneker's marginalia in his copy of *The Anatomy of Negation,* in the New York Public Library, includes: "Old Bob Ingersoll said that an honest god is the noblest work of man" (149). On page 149 Huneker also wrote "father" next to Ingersoll's name in the text.

Oscar Wilde called Ingersoll the most intelligent man in the United States during his 1882 lecture tour. See Lloyd Lewis and Henry Justin Smith, *Oscar Wilde Discovers America* (New York, 1936), p. 430.

14. Huneker, *Steeplejack,* II, p. 204. Huneker wrote in his copy of *The Anatomy of Negation,* "Bravo Edgar! A bully book."

15. *The Anatomy of Negation* (London, 1886), prefatory note, unpaged.

16. Eric L. McKitrick, "Decadence and Bohemianism in the 1890's," (History MA Thesis, Columbia University, January, 1951), p. 11.

17. *Anatomy,* p. 77.

18. *Ibid.,* pp. 103, 195, 223-24. Francis Saltus Saltus did not

believe in the divinity either. See letter to Brander Matthews, November 26, 1878. Columbia University.

19. R. A. A. in the London *Inquirer,* n.d., n.p.; Worcester *Daily Spy,* Saturday, June 20, 1885, n.p.; Julian Hawthorne, *The World,* Sunday, February 6, 1887, n.p. These reviews are in a scrapbook in the private collection of Elsie Welsh Saltus.

20. James Sully uses this phrase in his table of contents: *Pessimism* (London, 1877), p. xiv.

21. Thomas Mann, Introduction, *The Living Thoughts of Schopenhauer,* trans. Mrs. H. T. Lowe-Porter, (New York, 1939), p. 29.

22. *Philosophy,* pp. 100, 24, 161.

23. *Ibid.,* p. 161.

24. *Ibid.,* p. 227.

25. In *Love and Lore* (New York, 1890), pp. 50-51; originally published in *Lippincott's,* April, 1889, pp. 594-97.

26. *Ibid.,* pp. 52, 56, 57.

27. We cannot, however, ignore Saltus' shift from strong antitheism to a large embrace of whatever gods men have created. His earliest notebook has entries or copied-out material critical of godhead and Christianity. A later notebook accepts the existence of godhead. ESC, Yale.

28. *Lords of the Ghostland* (New York, 1907), pp. 65, 142.

29. "Our Note-book," *Collier's, XVII* (May 14, 1896), 6.

30. See Lewis Mumford, "The Revolt of the Demons," *New Yorker,* May 23, 1964, 155-85. Freud, of course, has an affinity with the "anti-rationalist element of the Romanticist tradition," as Lionel Trilling also noted in "Freud and Literature," *The Liberal Imagination* (New York, 1950), p. 49. Freud himself thought Schopenhauer anticipated his concept of the death wish.

Chapter Three

1. His one-act play *After the Ball,* published in *Smart Set,* LXVII (March, 1922), 93-99, is a light masquerade with a nostalgia for wealth, food, balls, and beauty and with cruelty and murder at its heart. The characters are phantoms as their names show; the woman is Diane des Baisers.

His poetry was published in *Poppies and Mandragora* (New York, 1926). (The volume contains twenty-three poems by Marie Saltus.) Mrs. Saltus chose the sonnets, the book title, the epigraph. (The notebook in which she found the epigraph to Barbey d'Aurevilly shows the words were more likely meant for one poem than for an entire book.) She found many of the poems in an early Saltus notebook;

the earliest dated one is 1883. The poems are almost always sonnets in the Italian form. Perhaps the best is the following:

THE FEAST

Below the glow of Guatemalan skies,
In groves where undergrass grows overgreen,
Where saffron quetzals from the branches lean,
And lilac lizards with basaltic eyes
Dart their vermilion tongue at fireflies
That gleam, in sudden loops of light between
The orchids and the fuchsias and their sheen—
Supremely there a spangled jaguar lies.
Curled in a velvet knot, the radiant beast
Sleeps on the vivid grass and sleeping dreams
That out beyond the brush and buds beneath,
Crouching he springs and knows again the feast;
The startled prey, the vain escape, the screams,
The Flesh that parts and bleeds between his teeth.

2. Van Vechten, "Edgar Saltus; A Postscript," p. 163.
3. *Mr. Incoul's Misadventure* (New York, 1887), p. 118.
4. *Ibid.*, pp. 89, 98. As interesting as this early use of a corrida in an American novel is Lenox Leigh's passion for Andalucia. Proudly acknowledging he has caught his passion from Theophile Gautier, Leigh hopes to re-visit his already adored Granada and Ronda. He is here surely the author's alter ego. In "Fabulous Andalucia," an essay in *Love and Lore*, Saltus traces the history of Andalucia from the Argonauts to the Arabs. *Incoul* also reflects some knowledge of the Basque country and an admiration for Goya that was to be life-long. Saltus is not included in Stanley T. Williams', *The Spanish Background of American Literature* (2 vols.; New Haven, 1955).
5. *Ibid.*, p. 99.
6. *Ibid.*
7. *The Truth About Tristrem Varick* (Chicago, 1888), pp. 32, 34.
8. *Ibid.*, p. 228.
9. *When Dreams Come True* (New York, 1895), p. 10. The name Jones, presumably chosen for its commonness, has its unexpected edge. Since the Joneses were an actual New York patrician family like the Rhinelanders and the Schermerhorns, "Keeping up with the Joneses" has its basis in actual social history.
10. *A Transaction in Hearts* (New York, 1889), p. 111.
11. *Ibid.*, p. 11.

12. Arthur Symons considers the English and Dutch mixture exotic and ascribes to it some of the responsibility for Saltus' odd quality. See "A Note on Edgar Saltus," p. 71.

13. *When Dreams Come True*, p. 8.

14. *Ibid.*, p. 171. The title of Tancred's first book, *Sonnets, Serene and Otherwise*, is precisely the title Saltus inscribed on his earliest extant notebook, probably begun some twelve years before *When Dreams Come True* was published. ESC, Yale.

15. *Enthralled* (*London, 1894*), unpaged; Chapter II, "The Beast and the Beauty."

16. *Ibid.*

17. *Ibid.*

18. *The Ghost Girl* (New York, 1922), pp. 196, 236.

19. *Vanity Square* (Philadelphia, 1906), pp. 26, 10-11.

20. *Ibid.*, pp. 5, 12.

21. *Ibid.*, pp. 38, 304.

22. *Daughters of the Rich* (New York, 1909), p. 54.

23. *The Monster* (New York, 1912), p. 175.

24. *Ibid.*, pp. 227-28.

25. From "A Transient Guest," in *A Transient Guest and Other Episodes* (Chicago, 1889), p. 51.

26. "The Dear Departed, in *Purple and Fine Women* (New York, 1903), p. 55.

27. "A Maid of Modern Athens," *Transient Guest*, pp. 40, 133.

28. Munson, "The Limbo of American Literature," p. 256. Saltus' unfinished and unpublished novel, *The Golden Flood*, has as its hero a society-bred reporter involved in a mysterious death. The *Ghost Girl* is also a kind of detective story. The number of trials in Saltus novels is high.

Chapter Four

1. John Davidson, *Earl Lavender* (London, 1895), p. 68; Carl Van Vechten, *The Tattooed Countess* (New York, 1924, 1963), p. 45 in 1963 edition. In the latter novel the Countess is asked: "Why were you tattooed? Is it fin de siècle?" The Countess replies, "Why, no, Lou; it's eternal." Even *Once A Week*, a Collier's publication, ran a little column called "Fin-de-Siècleisms" in the 1890's. The term obviously had great popular vogue and a variety of meanings.

2. Gorham Munson, "The Limbo of American Literature," p. 253.

3. "Our Note-book," *Collier's Weekly*, (April 16, 1898), 6. The original version appeared in the introduction to Barbey d'Aurevilly, *Story Without A Name* (New York, 1891), pp. 17-18.

4. Holbrook Jackson, *The Eighteen Nineties* (London, 1913), pp. 136, 138.

5. Saltus was to say more than once: "No grammarian ever wrote a thing that was fit to read." In "Truffles and Tokay," *Smart Set,* VI (April 1902), 68. Reprinted in the *Pomps of Satan.* See also the introduction to *Story Without A Name,* pp. 11-12.

6. "Our Note-book," *Collier's,* XVII (May 28, 1896), 6.

7. Arthur Symons, "The Decadent Movement in Literature," *Harper's,* LXXXVIII (November, 1893), 858-67. If Saltus found fault with Barbey d'Aurevilly's style, he may have been critical of Huysmans whom he also admired. He considered Barbey "very attackable" as a writer despite his genius. See the introduction to *Story Without A Name,* pp. 16-18, where Saltus also notices that Barbey never revised, that he lacked "that faculty which makes the purist, which made Flaubert."

8. "Along the Boulevards," *Once A Week, XL* (September 9, 1893), 7; and "Caviar and Champagne," *Ainslee's,* X (January, 1903), 117.

9. Jackson, *The Eighteen-Nineties,* pp. 137-38.

10. Letter, Wilde to Saltus, c. September, 1890, in *The Letters of Oscar Wilde,* ed. Rupert Hart-Davis (London, 1962), p. 670.

11. Notebook Two. ESC, Yale.

12. *Ibid.* Saltus elsewhere warns that "genius does not fall from the skies in evening dress. It took Balzac ten years to form a style that suited him, and almost as many more to form another that suited the public." From, "Saltusiana: On Crusts," *Once A Week,* XI (April 15, 1893), 7. Or, "Geniuses often write badly, and so much the better for them. At the same time, an inability to write well is not evidence of special talent, although true it is that a very large number of entirely amiable people think so." From "Our Note-book," *Collier's,* XIX (September 30, 1897), 7.

13. "The Passing of Guerrita," in "Men, Women and Events," *Cosmopolitan,* XXVIII (March, 1900), 515-16.

14. Carl Van Vechten and Gorham Munson both called Saltus a master of the short sentence. See Van Vechten in "Musk and Mortar," New York *Tribune,* September 10, 1922, n.p.; and Munson in "The Limbo of American Literature," p. 254.

15. Munson, "The Limbo of American Literature," p. 253. Not every reader thrilled to *Imperial Purple;* one unimpressed contemporary reviewer felt that "any book which, like this one, conceives of Imperial Rome as a succession of madmen and profligates soon wearies the imagination with its unreality." From anonymous news clipping from an unidentified London newspaper entitled "Imperial Purple Patches." ESC, Yale.

16. *Ibid.,* p. 254.

17. "Aloes and Ambrosia," *Uplands of Dream,* pp. 95-96; orig-

inally published in *Smart Set,* XV (January, 1905), 119-122. "Truffles and Tokay," *Pomps of Satan,* p. 108; originally in *Smart Set,* VI (April, 1902), 67-71.

18. "Human Hyenas," *Pomps of Satan,* p. 174.

19. "De l'Amour," *Pomps of Satan,* pp. 68-69. The laureate is identified as Robert Bridges in "Fifth Avenue," *Dress and Vanity Fair,* October 1913, p. 43.

20. H. B. Armitage, "Companion Piece to Salome," *Post,* n.d., n.u., mounted in a scrapbook. ESC, Yale.

21. *Enthralled,* unpaged, Chapter II, "The Beast and the Beauty." See discussion of the novel in Chapter III.

22. "Reflections of Floriline Schopenhauer," *Harper's Bazar,* XLIX (June, 1914), 20; XLVIII (November, 1913), 20. Saltus called the Floriline pieces one of his "minor turpitudes" in a letter to Van Vechten, February 27, 1918. VVC, Yale.

23. *Love and Lore,* p. 66.

24. Arthur Ganz, "The Meaning of *The Importance of Being Earnest,*" *Modern Drama,* VI (May, 1963), 45, 46.

25. Jackson, *The Eighteen-Nineties,* pp. 138, 139-40.

26. New York Evening *Sun,* June 28, 1906. Clipping mounted in a scrapbook in the possession of Elsie Welsh Saltus.

27. Hartmann, "The Edgar Saltus I Knew," pp. 18, 17.

28. Towne, "A Number of Things."

29. See "Our Note-book," *Collier's,* XVIII (October 8, 1896), 3.

30. *Pomps of Satan,* p. 151.

31. *Their Day in Court,* p. 89.

32. Quoted by Stanley Weintraub (ed.), *The Yellow Book* (New York, 1964), p. xix. The British writer frequently found his country as impossible for writers and writing as the American writer. R. L. Stevenson wrote to Richard Le Gallienne: "The little artificial popularity of style in England tends, I think, to die out; the British pig returns to his true love, the love of the styleless, of the shapeless, of the slapdash and the disorderly." Quoted in Le Gallienne's *The Romantic* 90's (London, 1951), p. 137. (First edition, 1926.)

33. Introduction to Barbey d'Aurevilly, *Story Without A Name* (New York, 1919), p. 19.

Chapter Five

1. In the form quoted the poem appears in *Love and Lore,* p. 81. Another version of the last line is: "To meet with Thoreau in the woods again." This version appears in a magazine clipping, source unknown, mounted in a scrapbook now at Yale. The poem appears in *Poppies and Mandragora* under the title, "A Memory"; in this version the last line reads: "To muse with Thoreau in the woods again!"

2. Letter, Saltus to Van Vechten, February 25, 1919. VVC, Yale. Saltus' first known published work is a libretto translation of *The Corsican Brothers* by Alexandre Dumas under the pseudonym of Gerardus Van Dam in 1883. His translations as well as his frequent notebook entries in French indicate his proficiency in the language.

3. *Ibid.* One review of *Balzac* delightfully comments, "The account is fragmentary, spasmodic, and jerky, and is in this respect altogether French." From the San Francisco *Weekly Bulletin,* n.d., n.p., ESC, Yale.

4. *Victor Hugo and Golgotha* (Chicago, 1925), pp. 6-7.

5. Letter, Saltus to Van Vechten, February 25, 1919. VVC, Yale.

6. *Victor Hugo and Golgotha,* p. 38.

7. See Bruce A. Morrissette, "Early English and American Critics of French Symbolism," in *Studies in Honor of Frederick W. Shipley. Washington University Studies, New Series. Language and Literature,* No. 14. (St. Louis, 1942), pp. 159-80. Saltus is not mentioned in this work.

8. Introduction to Balzac, *After Dinner Stories* (New York, 1886), p. 11.

9. *Ibid.,* p. 19.

10. For sample Saltus discussions of Zola see: *Collier's,* XX (March 12, 1898), 6; XXX (August 6, 1898), 2; *Once A Week,* XI (August 5, 1893), 6; *The Philosophy of Disenchantment,* p. 226.

11. See "Along the Boulevards," *Once A Week,* XI (July 22, 1893), 6. Many years later Kenneth Cornell in *The Post-Symbolist Period: French Poetic Currents, 1910-1920* (New Haven, 1958) corroborates the judgment that literary France was in transition near the end of the century. A questionnaire circulated by *l'Ermitage* among writers in 1901 showed Hugo still rated higher than any other nonliving French poet. See Chapter 1 and p. 24.

12. *Anatomy,* pp. 213, 215.

13. *Parnassians Personally Encountered,* (Cedar Rapids, Ia., 1923), p. 21.

14. *Ibid.,* pp. 21-22.

15. "Along the Boulevards," *Once A Week,* XI (August 19, 1893), 7. The anomaly is by now expected. Compare Jean Cocteau who, after a long career as an *enfant terrible,* accepted election to the Academy.

16. The classic earliest definition in English is Arthur Symons' in "The Decadent Movement in Literature." In this article Symons uses Decadent and Symbolist interchangeably. He does not discard the term Decadent for Symbolist until the publication of his book, *The Symbolist Movement in Literature* in 1899. See the preface to the recent re-issue of the Symons work (New York, 1958) in which he is

credited with naming the movement. It is worth noticing this evidence that the term *symbolist* had already replaced *decadent* in 1893 even for onlookers like Saltus.

17. Whitman was one of the passions of Huneker's youth. Francis Viélé-Griffin called himself "le petit-fils de Walt Whitman" according to Vance Thompson in *French Portraits* (Boston, 1899). Oscar Wilde paid two visits to Whitman during his 1882 tour of the United States. We may assume Saltus knew Whitman's work.

18. In his essay, "Morality in Fiction," in *Love and Lore,* Saltus believes only the grossest critical misunderstanding can label the *Scarlet Letter* and *Adam Bede* "unsuited to the Young Person," p. 69.

19. The comment on F. Marion Crawford is from a private notebook. ESC, Yale. The comment on Joaquin Miller is from *Parnassians Personally Encountered,* p. 11.

20. *Balzac,* p. 141. The comment comes from the chapter entitled "The Thinker" which merely lists wise excerpts from Balzac. Saltus was himself similarly searching for wise sayings by G. F. Monkshood in *Wit and Wisdom from Edgar Saltus* (London, 1903).

21. *Philosophy of Disenchantment,* p. 46 and undated, untitled newspaper article, c. 1900, in a scrapbook. ESC, Yale.

22. Letter, Saltus to Huneker, September 19, 1916. ESC, Yale.

23. *Victor Hugo and Golgotha,* p. 7.

24. "Our Note-book," *Collier's,* XX (December 16, 1897), 6; see also "Saltus on Erotic Literature," Chicago *Evening Post,* December 23, 1894, p. 4. Evidence that James and Saltus knew one another has not been uncovered. On the inside of the back cover of the notebook titled *Sonnets Serene and Otherwise* (c. 1883-1895), Saltus has copied out James's London address. He may have written to him or visited him.

Saltus is not unaware of Twain's value or his tradition. Once, for example, he laments the decline of American humor; except for Twain and "occasionally Colonel Roosevelt, there is no one to whom we can turn for it now." His lament for the passing of Petroleum Nasby, Billy Burch, Bill Nye, Josh Billings is not perfunctory. See "The Decline of American Humor," New York *Journal,* Sunday, November 18, 1900, n.p. ESC, Yale.

25. See R. H. Stoddard in the introduction to *Selections from Swinburne,* p. xvi, and T. E. Hulme in "Romanticism and Classicism" in *Speculations* (London, 1936), p. 125.

Apropos of gossip that Ruskin was being considered for the position of poet laureate, Saltus wrote: "No poet in England should accept the honor until it has been offered to and declined by Swinburne, than whom no mightier-mouthed inventor of harmonies has sung to

English ears." His other remarks on Ruskin show Saltus must have sided with Whistler against Ruskin in the first of the two famous literary libel suits of the 1890's. See "Pillar to Post," *Once A Week,* XI (June 3, 1893), 3.

26. Letter, Wilde to Saltus, c. September, 1890, *The Letters of Oscar Wilde,* p. 275.

27. According to Robert M. Limpus, "Not a word concerning Wilde's trial was published in the principal American magazines." See Limpus, *American Criticism of British Decadence, 1880-1890* (Chicago, 1939), p. 84.

28. *Oscar Wilde: An Idler's Impressions* (Chicago, 1917), p. 22. In a letter to Car Van Vechten, February 19, 1918, Saltus wrote, "Wilde based his play as I based my chapter [in *Mary Magdalen*] on the evocation which is contained in Flaubert's Trois Contes." VVC, Yale.

29. *Oscar Wilde,* pp. 25-26.

30. Letter, Harris to Saltus, September 18, 1918. ESC, Yale.

31. Notebooks Three and One. ESC, Yale.

32. "Why American Novels Are Flabby," *Anti-Philistine,* IV (September 15, 1897), 271.

33. "The Literary Industry" in "Men, Women and Events," *Cosmopolitan,* XXXIII (May, 1902), 106-7.

34. "Caviar and Champagne," *Ainslee's,* X (January, 1903), 117.

35. Melancthon Orr in *The Perfume of Eros* (New York, 1905), pp. 179-80.

36. "The Future of Fiction," *Love and Lore,* p. 42.

37. "Our Note-book," *Collier's,* XVII (July 16, 1896), 10.

38. "The Future of Fiction" and "Morality in Fiction" in *Love and Lore,* pp. 42, 73, 77.

39. "Saltus on Erotic Literature," Chicago *Evening Post,* December 23, 1891, p. 4.

40. "Caviar and Champagne," pp. 117-18.

41. "The Future of Fiction," "Morality in Fiction, "*Love and Lore,* pp. 45, 74.

42. "The Future of Fiction," *Love and Lore,* pp. 46-47. Saltus partly means by these statements that the novelist must be aware of the new psychology.

43. *Ibid.,* p. 45.

44. *Ibid.,* pp. 37-38.

45. Walter Blackburn Harte, *Anti-Philistine,* IV (September 15, 1897), 270, 271-72.

46. *Ibid.*, 276-77.

47. Saltus' remark is apropos of a discussion of D'Annunzio and Dostoevsky in "Along the Boulevards," *Once A Week*, XI (October 7, 1893), 6.

48. "Edgar Saltus' Methods," newsclipping dated 1891. ESC, Yale.

Chapter Six

1. Mario Praz, *The Romantic Agony* (New York, 1933, 1956), p. 1.

2. Letter, Saltus to Van Vechten, February 19, 1918. VVC, Yale.

3. *Imperial Purple*, pp. 70, 31, 202, 219.

4. *Ibid.*, p. 234.

5. Ruth Stephenson accords him this place; although Saltus "did not always have the original sources at his fingertips and although he did not always 'ascertain the severest truth,' as did Henry Charles Lea, he was still sufficiently rooted in the scientific approach to believe that history is something more than a series of conspicuous figureheads and events." See p. 164 in "Literary Techniques, Backgrounds, and Ideas of Edgar Saltus."

6. *Imperial Purple*, p. 92.

7. *Imperial Orgy*, pp. 193, 13, 51-52, 148, 184.

8. *Ibid.*, p. 162.

9. *Ibid.*, pp. 196, 236-37.

10. Ben Ray Redman, Introduction, *The Imperial Orgy* (New York, 1927), p. vi.

11. See, for example, "Our Note-book," *Collier's*, XI (September 16, 1893), 14; XI (April 29, 1893), 6; XVII (May 14, 1896), 6; XVII (May 21, 1896), 6; XVIII (December 3, 1896), 4; XXII (October 22, 1898), 11; "The Mystery of the Morgue," New York *Journal*, Sunday, May 17, 1896, p. 23.

12. "The Mystery of the Morgue." He used the same material in *Collier's*, XVII (May 21, 1896), 6. Saltus therefore wrote about his morgue visit twice within five days. In another *Collier's* column, XXII (February 18, 1899), 6, Saltus comments on a Mme. Ixe who with her three distinct personalities calls up Ovid and Charcot.

13. "Our Note-book," *Collier's*, XVII (May 14, 1896), 6.

14. "Human Hyenas," *Pomps of Satan*, p. 184. The growing power of the press, especially in its invasion of privacy, was one phenomenon of the period. Compare Henry James: "I have a morbid passion for personal privacy and a standing quarrel with the blundering publicities of the age." From *Letters*, ed. Percy Lubbock (New York, 1920) Letter to Howells, I, p. 203.

15. "Our Note-book," *Collier's,* XXI (May 7, 1898), 7. See also, XXI (August 27, 1898), 10-11, signed editorial and XXII (February 4, 1899), 6-7.

16. "Our Note-book," *Collier's,* XX (March 12, 1898), 6.

17. Signed editorial, *Collier's,* XXII (October 15, 1898), 2; XXII (December 10, 1898), 6; XXI (May 14, 1898), 19.

18. "Our Note-book," *Collier's,* XXII (March 25, 1899), 6; signed editorial, *Collier's,* XXI (August 27, 1898), 2.

19. "Our Note-book," *Collier's,* XXI (May 7, 1898), 19; XXI (August 27, 1898), 2; XXII (February 4, 1899), 6.

20. "The Bear in the China Shop," undated, unpaged news clipping in a scrapbook. ESC, Yale. See also *Collier's,* XXII (October 15, 1898), 2; XVII (June 25, 1896), 10; XXII (March 25, 1899. 6. Of Russia's role in China he quipped: "The Cossack is undecided whether to cut the pigtail from the heathen or the heathen from the pigtail." See *Collier's,* XXII (December 24, 1898), 7.

21. "The Bear in the China Shop."

22. "The Origin of the Crime," New York *Herald,* June 24, 1917, p. 12; "Hoch der Kaiser," n.d., n.p.; "Teuton Illusions and a Cure," New York *Herald,* 1917; "The Soul of the World," New York *Herald,* June 10, 1917; "Why We Are At War," New York *Herald,* May 18, 1917, p. 8. All these articles are mounted in a scrapbook. ESC, Yale. The remark about "Berlinese soprani" occurs in a three page MS called "The Pipes of Priapus" which probably was published as a newspaper piece. ESC, Yale.

23. "The Gospel of Gold," *Uplands,* p. 89; originally published in *Smart Set,* IV (July, 1901), 87-90.

24. *Ibid.*, p. 173. As Saltus had on occasion sounded the Naturalist note, so he had also sounded his horrified belief that true evil is social: "Evil, when it is real, is necessary; but when it is artificial it is not. Real evil is the handcraft of Satan. Artificial evil is the work of man. Its worst form is the result of social conditions. . . . There is the real enemy of mankind—not Satan, but the poverty which is suffered to exist, and which induces that toil. One of these days, or more exactly, one of these centuries, the present necessity for it will seem as horrible and as stupid as the doctrine of infant damnation." See his column in the New York *Journal,* c. 1902, mounted in a scrapbook. ESC, Yale.

In a January 23, 1903 column, "The Cure of Crime," for the same newspaper, Saltus connects crime with insanity: "Crime is an impulsion precisely as insanity is," and foresees the coming of "a more humanitarian view of the criminal." He then ironically shows that this view has already arrived in Wall Street between 10 and 3: "The views of the grafters are there quoted with respect, their tips are besought, and the size of their rake-off makes the mouths of the rest of us champagne."

25. *Ibid.*, pp. 173, 174.

26. "Our Note-book," *Collier's,* XXII (February 18, 1899), 6.

27. *Uplands,* pp. 9-26.

28. Editorial, *Collier's,* XXI (July 16, 1898), 2.

29. Jackson, *The Eighteen-Nineties,* pp. 52-3.

30. See Eric McKitrick, Chapter III, "Eighteen Hundred and Ninety Five," in "*Decadence* and Bohemianism in the 1890's."

Even Ambrose Bierce thought Wilde's name should not be mentioned before ladies. See *The Letters of Ambrose Bierce,* ed. Bertha C. Pope (San Francisco, 1922), p. 89.

31. Letter, Saltus to Van Vechten, February 25, 1919. VVC, Yale.

32. "The Courts of Love," *Love and Lore,* p. 19; the other relevant essay is "The Canons of Pure Courtesy," *Love and Lore,* pp. 21-34.

33. "De l'Amour," *Pomps of Satan,* pp. 78-79.

34. "Vanity Square," *Pomps of Satan,* pp. 2, 12, 13; originally published in *Smart Set,* IV (June, 1901), 71-75. See also: "Our Foreign Princesses," *Uplands,* pp. 207-216 and "The Heiress," *Love and Lore,* pp. 107-112. The latter was reprinted as "The American Heiress" in the *Anti-Philistine,* II (June 15, 1897), 7-10.

35. "The Mystery of Beauty," *Uplands,* p. 85.

36. "The Golden Fold," *Pomps of Satan,* p. 19; originally published in *Smart Set,* VII (May, 1902), 127-31 under the title, "Manhattan's Golden Fold." In a more serious moment Saltus wrote: "Brains, bank accounts and beauty make a sum total, not genteel merely, but ideal." This ideal "is the aristocracy the nation awaits, the kind America ought to have." See "The Gold Book," *Uplands,* p. 233; originally published in *Smart Set,* XIII (June, 1904), 95-98.

37. "The Mystery of Beauty" and "The Bankruptcy of Beauty" in *Uplands,* pp. 85-86, 184-85.

38. *Uplands,* pp. 165-76; originally published in *Smart Set,* IV (July, 1901), 87-90.

39. One study of the problem is Sebastian de Grazia, *Time, Work and Leisure* (New York, 1962).

40. "The Mystery of Beauty," "The Bankruptcy of Beauty," *Uplands,* pp. 86, 183.

41. "The Heart of Manhattan," *Uplands,* pp. 60, 65, 67, 70.

42. *Historia Amoris* (New York, 1906), pp. 184, 248-49.

43. *Ibid.*, p. 261.

44. *The Gardens of Aphrodite* (Philadelphia, 1920), p. 14.

45. "Along the Boulevards," *Once A Week,* XI (October 8, 1893), 6.

46. From an untitled, undated newspaper article. ESC, Yale. See also in *Hugh Hyrtl:* "that pomp of Satan, which we have agreed to call Etiquette," p. 22.

47. "Saltusian Crusts," *Once A Week,* XI (May 13, 1893), 6.

48. "Our Note-book," *Colliers,* XVIII (October 29, 1896), 3; *Pomps of Satan,* p. 90.

Afterword

1. Henry James, *The American Scene,* (New York, 1907, 1946), p. 114 in the 1946 edition.

2. Matthew Josephson, *Portrait of the Artist as American* (New York, 1930), p. 289.

3. Grant Overton, "Now About This Fellow Saltus," *Bookman,* LXI (August, 1925), 646.

4. Alfred Kazin, *On Native Grounds* (New York, 1942, 1956), p. 45.

5. As Harry Levin put it, the results of the period "may be counted in educated audiences, rather than achieved masterpieces." "The Discovery of Bohemia," *Literary History of the United States,* ed. Robert E. Spiller, *et al.* (New York, 1946, 1960), p. 1077.

6. William Gaunt reminds us that the *Penny Encyclopedia* of 1832 considers "esthetics" a German-derived term. For some time "esthetics" was to seem German property. See *The Aesthetic Adventure* (New York, 1945), p. 11.

7. *When Dreams Come True,* p. 84.

8. James, *The American Scene,* p. 159.

9. See "Our Note-book," *Collier's Weekly,* XVIII (October 29, 1896), 6.

10. Sunday, November 29, 1896, p. 29. The New York *Journal* may not have been so unlikely a location for allusions to Huysmans. Stephen Crane shared space in the October 25, 1896 issue with Saltus. His contribution was, "The Tenderloin as it Really Is." These articles appeared during Hearst's ownership of the *Journal.* The first anniversary issue, Sunday, November 8, 1896, contained greetings from the paper's literary contributors, among them William Dean Howells and Julian Hawthorne as well as Saltus and Crane.

11. Notebook Three. ESC, Yale.

12. *The Monster,* p. 13.

13. Notebook Two. ESC, Yale.

Selected Bibliography

UNPUBLISHED AND UNCOLLECTED SALTUS MATERIAL

The basic collection, donated by Carl Van Vechten and Elsie Welsh Saltus, is part of the Collection of American Literature at Yale University. It includes manuscripts, letters, uncollected essays, clippings, notebooks, memorabilia and other material.

Other important holdings are at the University of Virginia (the Clifton Waller Barrett Collection), Columbia University (the Brander Matthews Collection), the Henry E. Huntington Library and in the private collections of Elsie Welsh Saltus and Charles Honce.

PRIMARY SOURCES

The Saltus listing omits the Collier compilations, miscellaneous pieces, and uncollected columns and essays that appeared in periodicals like *Once A Week, Collier's, Harper's Bazar, Lippincott's, Puck, Forum, Munsey's, Hearst's, Ainslee's, The Wave, Anti-Philistine, Dress and Vanity Fair, Cosmopolitan, Smart Set,* and numerous newspaper articles. Some of them are referred to in Notes and References; a number of the essays have been collected in *Love and Lore, The Pomps of Satan* and *The Uplands of Dream.*

For a listing that includes the Collier "brats" and other miscellaneous items, see Jacob Blanck, *Merle Johnson's American First Editions,* Fourth Edition, (New York, 1942). The fullest annotated bibliography is probably the private unpublished one by Charles Honce.

The AMS Press, Inc. is reprinting those works of Saltus which are preceded by an asterisk.

1. *Fiction*

**Mr. Incoul's Misadventure.* New York: Benjamin and Bell, 1887.
**The Truth About Tristrem Varick.* Chicago: Belford, Clarke, 1888.
**Eden.* Chicago: Belford, Clark, 1888.
**A Transaction in Hearts.* New York: Belford, Clarke, 1889.
**A Transient Guest and Other Episodes.* New York: Belford, Clarke, 1889.
**The Pace That Kills.* Chicago: Belford, Clarke, 1889.
**Mary Magdalen.* New York: Belford, 1891.

The Facts In The Curious Case of Hugh Hyrtl, Esq. New York: P. F. Collier, 1892.
Madam Sapphira. New York: F. Tennyson Neely, 1893.
Enthralled. London: Tudor Press, 1894.
When Dreams Come True. New York: P. F. Collier, 1895.
Purple and Fine Women. New York; Ainslee, 1903.
The Perfume of Eros. New York: A. Wessels, 1905.
Vanity Square. Philadelphia: Lippincott, 1906.
Daughters of the Rich. New York: Mitchell Kennerley, 1909.
The Monster. New York: Pulitzer, 1912.
The Paliser Case. New York: Boni and Liveright, 1919.
The Ghost Girl. New York: Boni and Liveright, 1922.

2. *Poetry*

Poppies and Mandragora. Poems by Edgar Saltus, with 23 additional poems by Marie Saltus. New York: Harold Vinal, 1926.

3. *History, Philosophy, Essays*

Balzac. Boston: Houghton, Mifflin. 1884.
The Philosophy of Disenchantment. New York: Belford, 1885.
The Anatomy of Negation. London: Williams and Norgate, 1886.
Love and Lore. New York: Belford, 1890.
Imperial Purple. Chicago: Morrill, Higgins, 1892.
The Pomps of Satan. London: Greening, 1904.
Historia Amoris. New York: Mitchell Kennerley, 1906.
The Lords of the Ghostland. New York: Mitchell Kennerley, 1907
Oscar Wilde: An Idler's Impression. Chicago: Brothers of the Book, 1917. (Privately printed.)
The Imperial Orgy. New York: Boni and Liveright, 1920.
The Gardens of Aphrodite. Philadelphia: Pennell Club, 1920. (Privately printed.)
Parnassians Personally Encountered. Cedar Rapids: Torch Press, 1923.
The Uplands of Dream, ed. Charles Honce. Chicago: Pascal Covici, 1925.
Victor Hugo and Golgotha. Chicago: Pascal Covici, 1925.

4. *Translations*

Balzac: After-Dinner Stories. Trans. by Myndart Verelst. New York: George J. Coombes, 1886.
*Mérimée, Prosper and Théophile Gautier. *Tales Before Supper.* Englished by Myndart Verelst. New York: Brentano's, 1887.
Barbey d'Aurevilly. *Story Without A Name.* Chicago: Belford, 1891; New York: Brentano's, 1919 (with a new introduction).

SELECTED SECONDARY SOURCES

Criticism about Edgar Saltus exists primarily in book reviews and in brief magazine articles very few of which have survived their occasional character.

BROOKS, VAN WYCK. *The Confident Years, 1885-1915*. New York: Dutton, 1952. Treats Saltus as an upper class New Yorker, dandy, and hedonist whose fantastic New York was soon to become real in Edith Wharton's novels.

CARTER, JOHN. "Saltus is Saltus After All," New York *Times*, June 14, 1925, sec. 3, p. 11. Better than most journalistic criticism; an example of the critical reaction to the Brentano reprints. His final estimate—that Saltus had "no substance, only style."

DE CASSERES, BENJAMIN. "Edgar Saltus," *Forty Immortals*. New York: Seven Arts, 1926. Rapturous, hyperbolic appreciation.

COLLES, RAMSEY. "A Publicist: Edgar Saltus," *Westminster Review*, CLXII (October, 1904), 464-74. More admiration and summary than criticism from an English admirer.

HARTMANN, SADAKICHI. "The Edgar Saltus I Knew," *Bookman*, LVIII (September, 1923), 17-19. The best creation there is of Saltus as legendary recluse and dandy, presumably from firsthand knowledge of Saltus at Edgar Fawcett's Friday evenings in the early 1890's.

HICKS, GRANVILLE. "Edgar Saltus," *Dictionary of American Biography*. XVI. New York: Scribners, 1935. Saltus presented for his historical rather than his literary importance.

HUBBARD, ELBERT. "Heart to Heart Talks with Philistines by the Pastor of His Flock." *Philistine*, XXV (October, 1907), 129-43. Another curmudgeon of the period praises Saltus for his style: "It's all like a cherry in a morning Martini."

HUNEKER, JAMES G. *Steeplejack*. New York: Scribner's, 1923. The best primary reminiscence by a contemporary author and friend.

JACKSON, HOLBROOK. *The Eighteen-Nineties*. London: Jonathan Cape, 1913. A classic history of the English esthetes, indispensable to the student of the American *fin de siècle* as a basis for comparison between the two movements.

KITCHEN, PAUL H. "Sorceror of Syllabus," *Open Road*, XLIII (March-April 1, 1943), 15-17. Interesting chiefly for the late date of its appearance; repeats the legend of the Saltus preciosity, extols his style, and laments his decline.

LEVIN, HARRY. "The Discovery of Bohemia," *Literary History of the United States,* ed. Robert E. Spiller and others. New York: Macmillan, 1953. The finest brief study; responsive to the comedy and irony in Saltus.

LIMPUS, ROBERT M. *American Criticism of British Decadence.* Portion of a Ph.D. thesis, University of Chicago, 1939. The only survey of the American reception of the English esthetes.

MCKITRICK, ERIC. "Decadence and Bohemianism in the 1890's." Unpublished M.A. thesis, Columbia University, January 1951. The American analogue to Holbrook Jackson's work; an excellent examination of little magazines, editors, and writers of the period.

———. "Edgar Saltus of the Obsolete," *American Quarterly,* III (Spring, 1951), 22-35. This published revision of the chapter on Saltus in the author's master's essay is thorough, incisive and indispensable.

MENCKEN, H. L. "Edgar Saltus." *Prejudices: Fifth Series.* New York: Knopf, 1926. Occasioned by the Marie Saltus biography and published originally in the New York *World,* October 11, 1925, the article assumes the "complete collapse" of a "shining star." These extremes are less surprising than Mencken's uncritical acceptance of the biography.

MORRISSETTE, BRUCE A. "Early English and American Critics of French Symbolism." *Studies in Honor of Frederick W. Shipley. Washington University Studies. New Series. Language and Literature No. 14.* St. Louis: Washington University, 1942, pp. 159-80. In this important effort, Saltus' scattered comments receive no mention; the work begun here needs to be continued.

MUNSON, GORHAM. "The Limbo of American Literature." *Broom,* II (June, 1922), 250-60. A good example of the use of Saltus in the 1920's to document American cultural limitations.

POLLARD, PERCIVAL. *Their Day in Court.* New York: Neale, 1909. A lively contemporary finds Saltus addicted "to the sentence that glitters yet is not gold," but still insists that American writers need to develop a concern for style.

SALTUS, MARIE. *Edgar Saltus: The Man.* Chicago: Pascal Covici, 1925. Has some value but cannot be considered a portrait of Saltus during his best writing years; more than half of the work deals with Saltus during the last ten to fifteen years of his life.

———. "Letter to the Editor," *Bookman,* LVIII (January, 1924), 597-98. Important for its rebuttal of Hartmann's version of Saltus; denies that Saltus knew Chinese, maintained an oriental salon and testifies instead to his much simpler habits of living.

SPRAGUE, CLAIRE. "The Edgar Saltus Collection," *Yale University Library Gazette,* XLII (October, 1967), 102-106. A description of the Elsie Welsh Saltus donation and a brief, critical introduction to Edgar's life and works.

STEPHENSON, RUTH E. "Literary Techniques, Background and Ideas of Edgar Saltus." Ph. D. thesis, University of Wisconsin, 1953. After careful study, the author concludes that Saltus stands alone in the American tradition, showing only some kinship with James Cabell and Joseph Hergesheimer. Especially interesting is the author's effort to relate her subject to American historical and philosophic thought of his era.

"The Stylist Who Created a Mythology of Manhattan," *Current Opinion,* LXV (October, 1918), 254-55. Its only interest lies in its suggestive title.

SULLY, JAMES. *Pessimism: A History and a Criticism.* London: Henry S. King, 1877. Standard English work on pessimism which Saltus knew; points up the popular—perhaps more properly, amateur—and literary character of the Saltus works on the subject.

SYMONS, ARTHUR. "A Note on Edgar Saltus," *Vanity Fair,* XIV (March, 1920). Brief, mixed appreciation of several novels, *Imperial Purple,* and *Oscar Wilde;* interesting more because it is by Symons than because it is good criticism.

———. "Edgar Saltus," *Dramatis Personae.* Indianapolis: Bobbs-Merrill, 1923. A reprint, with minor alterations, of the *Vanity Fair* article.

———. "The Decadent Movement in Literature," *Harper's* LXXXXVI (November, 1893), 858-67. Credited with defining the Symbolist movement for English readers, the article is a must for anyone interested in the 1890's on either side of the Atlantic; describes the French movement (Verlaine, Mallarmé and others) to the uninitiated.

TOWNE, CHARLES HANSON. "A Number of Things." Clipping from a New York Hearst newspaper, c. 1921; in the possession of Elsie Welsh Saltus. Reprinted, with minor alterations, in *Adventures in Editing.* New York: Appleton, 1926. Significant for its testimony that Saltus wrote slowly and revised little.

VAN DOREN, CARL. "The Roving Critic." *Nation,* CXIV (January 11, 1922), 45. Succinct, effective appreciation of Saltus' career as "the Satanist of America."

VAN VECHTEN, CARL. "Edgar Saltus," *The Merry-go-round.* New York: Knopf, 1918. Essentially expository appreciation.

———. "Edgar Saltus: A Postscript," *Double Dealer,* II (October, 1921), 162-64. Written shortly after Saltus died; reviews the reputation and works of "another illustrious obscurity" who will ultimately find a place between Poe and Howells in the American literary pantheon.

———. "Edgar Saltus in his Socks," *Herald Tribune Books,* October 11, 1925, p. 4. In this review of Marie Saltus' biography, the writer accepts the picture of Saltus as a neurotic recluse.

———. "Edgar Saltus." *Excavations.* New York: Knopf, 1926. Alteration and expansion of the 1918 *Merry-go-round* essay.

WARNER, REV. BEVERLEY E. "Practical Pessimism," *New Englander,* XLVIII (June, 1888), 432-42. The only full-length discussion of Saltus in the 1880's I have found; discusses the two works on pessimism as clear expositions of a fashionable and immature point of view.

Index